THE
VITAL
PARTNERSHIP

To James Kitfield —

In acknowledgment of his vital

contributions to our understanding

of the transatlantic partnership

& with friendship —

THE
VITAL
PARTNERSHIP

POWER AND ORDER

AMERICA AND EUROPE BEYOND IRAQ

SIMON SERFATY

ROWMAN & LITTLEFIELD PUBLISHERS, INC.
Lanham • Boulder • New York • Toronto • Oxford

ROWMAN & LITTLEFIELD PUBLISHERS, INC.

Published in the United States of America
by Rowman & Littlefield Publishers, Inc.
A wholly owned subsidiary of The Rowman & Littlefield Publishing Group, Inc.
4501 Forbes Boulevard, Suite 200, Lanham, Maryland 20706
www.rowmanlittlefield.com

PO Box 317
Oxford
OX2 9RU, UK

British Library Cataloguing in Publication Information Available

Library of Congress Cataloging-in-Publication Data

Serfaty, Simon
  The vital partnership : power and order / Simon Serfaty.
    p. cm.
  Includes bibliographical references and index.
  ISBN 0-7425-4885-6 (cloth : alk. paper)
  1. European Union countries—Foreign relations—United States. 2. United States—
Foreign relations—European Union countries. I. Title.
  JZ1570.A57U67 2005
  327.7304—dc22   2005001995

Printed in the United States of America

♾™ The paper used in this publication meets the minimum requirements of
American National Standard for Information Sciences—Permanence of Paper
for Printed Library Materials, ANSI/NISO Z39.48-1992.

To Gail
My vital partner

CONTENTS

FOREWORD

Brent R. Scowcroft

I have vivid memories of the fall of 1989 when history surprised us all once more, when the Cold War seemed all of a sudden about to end, leaving us numb and disbelieving as we watched tens of thousands of German citizens "tear down that wall" in Berlin. There was also much hidden joy and pride during that moment: joy over the irrepressible hunger for freedom we were witnessing, but also pride for the role played by the United States after World War II, when it had made the commitments of leadership and power needed to help the democratic countries of Europe rebuild and rethink themselves to elude the lingering shadow of another Versailles. Less than two years after the reunification of Germany, another epochal event—the disintegration of the Soviet Union— confirmed that the end of an era had indeed come, and that the Cold War was over at last.

This book is not a comprehensive history of what brought us, America and Europe, to this point, from President Harry Truman's visionary decisions to the conclusive moments managed by President George H. W. Bush more than four decades later. But it is a thorough and refreshingly balanced assessment of the bold ideas that conditioned the U.S. return to the Old World, which Americans had left to start anew, and the transformation of the Old World, which two catastrophic wars in barely more than one generation had left in total disarray. It is also a compelling account of the rise of a partnership that gave both sides of the Atlantic the power and the will that each might have otherwise lacked to wage and win the Cold War.

That this "vital partnership" might be sliding toward estrangement is concern enough to make renewal a central goal for the next few years. Admittedly, returning to the transatlantic intimacy we enjoyed in earlier years will not be easy. The mutual unease we seem to feel toward each other transcends the personal or bilateral frictions that have been especially apparent over the war in Iraq and its difficult aftermath. The tensions run deeper and, paradoxically, reflect not only how far we have come together during the latter part of the past century, but also how much remains to be done in coming years.

The patterns of power and weaknesses that define the transatlantic partnership are hardly new. Throughout the Cold War, even as the countries of Europe were proceeding with their remarkable transformation, we often worried about the nagging military capability gap that stood between us, and by the troubling tendency for many in Europe to use the United States as a scapegoat for their limitations and a rallying cry for their unity. After 1991, military expenditures were cut sharply on both sides of the Atlantic, but the cuts in Europe proved much more extensive, and even before the war in Afghanistan, the conflicts in Bosnia and Kosovo had already shown unmistakably that an ever wider gap in usable capabilities was hampering NATO's ability to operate in an integrated fashion. Whether Europe will build the needed capabilities, and how these will be used if and when they become available, remains to be seen. The test will not be merely one of will but also one of efficacy.

A second issue relates to the dramatic transformation of Europe into the European Union (EU). As Simon Serfaty notes in the pages that follow, "Historians will marvel." On occasion, we in the United States have failed to understand fully the historic enormity of what the Europeans have achieved during the latter part of the past century, thus making our dialogue with our changed and changing partners unnecessarily difficult, sometimes acrimonious, and even occasionally petty. This has been true especially in the economic and trade areas, but increasingly in the political and security areas as well. Yet this has not been a one-way street either, and our friends in Europe, too, have often failed to appreciate in full the multidimensional U.S. contributions to their efforts. In thinking about the future of U.S.-EU relations within a renewed transatlantic partnership, we also have, therefore, a test of will combined with a test of efficacy. We need the will to organize our relations in ways that reflect the influence of Europe and its Union in the world, and the efficacy of mobilizing an Atlantic Community that remains the central depository of values most of the world now seeks, and the economic and military resources on which global security must rest.

These questions, which were already emerging at the end of the Cold War, have been greatly complicated by the horrific events of September 11. Whether the world was directly changed by these events, and how, can be debated, but these events did change America's view of the world and, partly as a consequence, the world's view of America. Now many of our like-minded partners in Europe seem to find us unilateral and indifferent, if not arrogant and even dismissive. It is important for them to understand the new sense of threat felt in America, but that understanding will come more readily if the United States pursues a multilateral framework that makes room for a warm, cooperative, and even on occasion tolerant relationship with its vital partners in Europe.

As we address the demanding and complex agenda that conditions our ongoing war on global terrorism, we will have to restore the cooperative faith we used to have in one another. That will demand considerable effort and may often entail significant frustration. But we can no more succeed in our present campaign by acting unilaterally than we could have in 1950 or in 1990. If anything, the challenges we now face make us even more in need of allies and friends than we were then, in Korea or in the Gulf. What Simon Serfaty does in this book is to point to the test of vision that looms ahead: to strengthen the Atlantic community of shared interests and compatible values, which was developed during the latter part of the past century, and extend it into the community of complementary actions required for the many issues that were left behind. Predictably, this book alone will not provide the will that is needed on both sides of the Atlantic to meet that test. But it can surely add to the understanding that meeting that test is an urgent priority that is all the more within our reach as our differences still remain relatively small.

Brent R. Scowcroft

ACKNOWLEDGMENTS

Any book, whatever its topic or its length, owes too much to too many for any acknowledgment of the author's debt to be complete. Thus, and as a matter of course, thanks should first go to every author named in the bibliography attached to the end of this book—and countless others who are not listed explicitly but form an implicit part of my intellectual memories. Thanks should also go to my colleagues at Old Dominion University (ODU) in Norfolk, Virginia, and at the Center of Strategic & International Studies (CSIS) in Washington, D.C., who contributed ideas and conversations over the past ten years, and to whom I am indebted. Thanks also go to the many graduate students who populated my seminars at ODU, and whose interests and curiosity sustained my own commitment to the subject matter.

Beyond these many good people, too numerous to be named individually, there are a few individuals I would like to single out for their interest in, and contributions to, this book. Odile Jacob and Bernard Gotlieb initially talked me into writing an essay on the evolution of U.S. policies since September 11, 2001, with emphasis on U.S. relations with Europe. Better yet, as evidence of her persuasive power, Odile Jacob convinced me to write this essay directly in French, which the superb publishing company that bears her name released in February 2004 as *La tentation impériale*. This book is certainly not a translation—both of these languages are simply not interchangeable—but many of the themes developed in *La tentation* reappear here, and I am grateful to Odile Jacob for her authorization to do so.

A number of friends read this manuscript, in part or in full, but two of them deserve special thanks. Marten van Heuven, a retired Foreign Service Officer and now a senior consultant at the Rand Corporation, is an outstanding observer of the never-ending saga of transatlantic relations. He is also an extraordinarily thorough (and occasionally demanding) reader, and I thank him for his many useful and always constructive comments. Seyom Brown, at Brandeis University, is a scholar's scholar, and over the years his work has shaped the study of U.S. foreign policy and world politics for countless students who found his many books to be the instructor's required reading. His generous comments and effective suggestions also helped complete and improve this book.

There are many others to thank, including two presidents—John Hamre, whose leadership at CSIS has confirmed the Center's substantive saliency as a premier think tank in Washington, D.C., and Craig Kennedy, at the German Marshall Fund of the United States, whose personal friendship and institutional support I have enjoyed for the past many years. Thanks, too, to Michelle Sparkman, my young colleague at CSIS, for her many contributions and reliable support.

As I look back at my professional life, I feel a special debt to the work that influenced me early on, and to which I returned as I wrote these pages—the work of Robert W. Tucker and George Liska, my two professors at the Johns Hopkins University in Baltimore, Maryland. Many of their books have been in print for a long time now. During and after the difficult and agonizing debate over the Vietnam War, they both engaged in an extraordinarily lively dialogue with elaborate essays that still read exceptionally well to this day, thirty to forty years later. They both were—are—men of unusual integrity; they did not compromise their scholarly vocation on behalf of elusive policy ambitions. Their reward is that their work has endured the merciless test of time, and I suspect that it will continue to be the case for other generations of students. In this sense, this modest essay is informally dedicated to them, respectfully.

My earlier book, *La tentation impériale*, was dedicated to my son, Alexis, who was then completing his graduate degree at Sciences Po' in Paris, France. The formal dedication for this book goes to my wife, Gail, whose presence, patience, and intelligence made her a truly vital partner.

December 1, 2004

INTRODUCTION

That relations between the United States and the states of Europe have been radically transformed over the past fifty years is certain. Each in its own and separate ways, America and Europe have bid farewell to their yesteryear.[1] To appreciate the scope of this transformation—America relative to Europe, and Europe relative to itself—demands a retroactive logic that reminds us of what has ceased to be, after two dehumanizing world wars brought the states of Europe progressively back to their senses while the Cold War was bringing America back to Europe.[2]

Yet, barely into the twenty-first century, the transatlantic partnership developed at the invitation of a large number of European countries, and a European union of states built with U.S. support, are questioned. On both sides of the Atlantic, complaints have become more vocal and calls for new partners more urgent. This is a critical juncture, and the next four years, 2005–2009, will be a defining moment. They parallel President Harry S. Truman's full term in office, beginning in January 1949, when after three years of a difficult introduction to the postwar security normalcy that had emerged after the horrific end of World War II, in August 1945, decisions and the events that prompted them were to shape the history of the next four decades. Now, too, a newly reelected U.S. president and his counterparts in Europe have a blind date with history—in March 2007, for the fiftieth anniversary of the Rome Treaties that launched the European Community, now a Union, and in April 2009, for the sixtieth anniversary of the Washington Treaty that launched the Atlantic Alliance.

What either Europe or the Alliance might look like when the time comes is not clear; what is clear, however, is that neither will stand still, for the better or for the worse.

For nearly half a century, the U.S. commitment to the institutional transformation of an ever closer and ever large Europe was steadfast and decisive. That commitment was often extended at some economic or political cost to the United States, but these costs were nonetheless justified by broader goals in and beyond Europe. Over the years, Europe's transformation also depended on four other conditions:

- Robust, sustained, and widely shared economic growth, often with the initial benefits going to the smaller and more needy economies;
- Stable and confident centrist national leadership able to resist pressures from either political extreme;
- Especially close ties between at least two European states acting as an internal locomotive for the other community members; and
- Regional stability east of Germany but also, and even before September 11, 2001, south of the Mediterranean.

These conditions were still met effectively during the post–Cold War years, when EU membership was expanded, institutions were reformed, and a single currency was launched. More recently, however:

- Economic growth has been below potential, and prospects for sustained recovery in the euro-zone are below the levels expected elsewhere in coming years. The EU agenda for specific and credible reforms to complete the single market and respond to the competitive challenges of globalization is stalled. Demographic conditions are potentially catastrophic, and public attitudes toward the much-needed immigrants who could compensate for Europe's depopulation are often hostile. In a context of painful economic rigor and widespread ambivalence over an increasingly visible institutional or "foreign" intrusion, public opinion polls reveal much unease with, and even anger about, the EU.
- As government choices respond to institutional decisions over which local constituencies have little influence, "Europe" is viewed as an ob-

stacle to the citizens' right to be represented by their democratically elected representatives. Frustrated by the alleged neglect of their interests and priorities, voters are turning against incumbent majorities. In 2004, governments that had been deemed to be strong before they followed the United States in Iraq were unexpectedly voted out of office (in Spain), dramatically weakened (in Great Britain), or were left at the mercy of the next election (in Poland and Italy). Concomitantly, weak governments that opposed the war grew weaker (including in Germany and France) notwithstanding widespread public support for their policies in Iraq and, even more widely, toward the United States. Whatever the case, such political volatility opens the door to expedient populist appeals from either extreme of the political spectrum; whether aimed at Europe proper, or protective of Europe at the expense of America, such appeals would be significant for both Europe's future and the future of its relations with the United States.

- Neither Germany nor France nor their respective political leaders show a capacity for the co-management of Europe, as was the case during the previous decade, not only because of the internal conditions faced by each of these countries but also because of new differences in their respective visions of Europe's future—what it should be and what it ought to do, how, and with whom. No less importantly, even when these differences are accommodated, other EU members have grown more hostile to any such bilateral control of their institutions. Looking ahead, Europe's political dynamism, especially with regard to its final foreign policy and security dimensions, will depend on the enlargement of its bilateral hard core to other members, including Great Britain, not only on political grounds (to reassure other EU countries that might otherwise fear a drift of their Union away from the United States) but also for military weight.[3] In short, the time is long gone when Britain could stay at the margin of Europe because of its ties with the United States, and when it might make sense for France to keep Britain away from the European institutions as an unwanted American "Trojan horse."

- Europe's new insecurity grows out of its vulnerability to acts of terror because of its geographic proximity, economic dependence, and political sensitivity to countries south of the Mediterranean where these acts might originate or from which they might be inspired. A wave of terrorism anywhere in Europe would quickly affect the national and institutional agendas everywhere else—as happened after the first oil crisis and related Middle East War in 1973, and again after the second oil crisis and the crisis in Iran between 1979 and 1983. In Spain in March 2004, a single act of terror, improvised in a few weeks by Spanish citizens of Moroccan origin, was enough to topple the governing majority and transform radically the dynamics of political relations within the EU. With the mythical "Arab streets" now no less significant in the national capitals of Old Europe than in the Middle East, the political consequences of disruptions imported from, or attributed to, "foreign" communities are potentially troubling.

Support for European unity is no longer reliable in the United States, where Europe is said to have lost its geopolitical significance relative to other parts of the world that either harbor the main threats to U.S. security or might provide the main opportunities for significant economic growth. But in Europe, too, America is said to be losing much of its relevance, especially in the Muslim world where are found the main areas of European security concerns (and, arguably, a renewed geopolitical center of Europe's influence). In 2004, George W. Bush was a convenient but misleading explanation for this pervasive drift—an alibi that Europeans used to object to policies that the U.S. president understandably refused to submit to the allies' test of acquiescence in the face of such open hostility. Looking ahead, during and beyond the second Bush administration, public conditions on both sides of the Atlantic may turn worse as younger elites that are not fully aware of the defining transformations of the Cold War lose their taste for cooperation, within Europe and with the United States, and their respective governments lose their new habits of consultation and cooperation and regain past habits of indifference or worse.

While the states of Europe debate what sort of a future they will have within the Union if they give the Union a future of its own, the next four years will also be a delicate moment for the future of Europe's alliance with the United States. Indeed, in 2005 the allies' ability to restore the transatlantic partnership will be challenged by two and a half wars that are as urgent as they are contentious.

Iraq is the first of these wars. Whether this was a war of choice or a war of necessity can be argued on moral and on security grounds; but ending the war honorably responds to both a moral and a security imperative that cannot be ignored. Unlike Vietnam, where the fear of failure reflected a frame of mind that bore little resemblance to reality, the consequences of failure in Iraq are sufficiently real to all to make them unacceptable for all.[4]

In 2004, even as it became increasingly apparent that the coalition assembled for Iraq's liberation from its oppressive regime was not up to the postwar missions of occupation, rehabilitation, reconstruction, and reconciliation, U.S. calls for an enlargement of the coalition of the willing remained largely ignored by the European allies who had relied on the United Nations to organize a global coalition of the discontent. With the U.S. election out of the way, additional contributions from the EU and their respective members, as well as additional NATO involvement, can no longer be delayed. Iraq was a failure for Europe even before it threatened to become America's failure: in 2002, because the states of Europe could not prevent a war they feared more than they feared Iraq; in 2003, because the proactive opposition shown by many of them harmed the goals they shared with the coalition of the willing; and in 2004, because having played a marginal role, or less, in liberating Iraq from Saddam Hussein's tyranny, they played no role in reconstructing and transforming that country away from his disastrous legacies.

It is true that the U.S. planning for war was contemptuous of the allies, while planning for postwar Iraq was pitifully insufficient—so wishful in its conception as to border on self-deception, so ineffective in its execution as to spell incompetence, and so stubborn in its defense as to suggest deception. Even if the coalition's removal of Saddam made the United States safer, notwithstanding his marginal relevance to the specific events of September 11, its inability to stabilize Iraq probably made the states of Europe less safe.[5] It is therefore a matter of self-interest for all EU and NATO members to be more engaged in that country—not merely to help the United States and the few capable countries that joined the coalition in 2003, but to help themselves. In 2005, the goal should be to negotiate the withdrawal of the coalition forces by a date that only a democratically elected Iraqi government can make certain, following a "decent interval" during which the rehabilitation of the Iraqi state would parallel visible progress in achieving domestic security and providing for political stability and economic affluence.

Afghanistan is the second of these wars. Apart from the United States, NATO countries have 1.2 to 1.5 million men in arms; their equipment earmarked for NATO includes 13,000 tanks, 35,000 armored infantry vehicles, and 11,000 aircrafts. Yet, in spite of President Karzai's plea at the NATO Summit in Istanbul, Turkey, in June 2004 "to please hurry, as NATO in Afghanistan . . . today and not tomorrow," the European members of NATO could not send the 3,500 to 4,000 troops requested by Karzai for the then-upcoming national elections of October 9, 2004. When agreement for additional forces was reached later that summer (about half of what the Afghan president had requested), deployment was limited to two months in spite of worsening security conditions outside Kabul. Unlike Iraq, since the end of major combat operations in early 2002, the test in Afghanistan has not been over a U.S. willingness to act with Europe and NATO. What has been tested instead is NATO's ability to act even when America is willing to wait for additional European contributions as long as needed (which had not been the case in late 2001). Without a substantial increase in security assistance from NATO and its members, the Afghan elections will not suffice to bring stability to the entire country. In short, Afghanistan goes to the heart of NATO's credibility for future conflicts, especially as in Afghanistan, unlike elsewhere, there are no serious policy divisions within the Alliance as well as within Europe.

Finally, one to three years away from having nuclear weapons capacity, Iran is a decisive challenge that will measure the relevance of the EU in the United States and that of the alliance in Europe. That Iraq did not have weapons of mass destruction, as had been widely assumed before the war, does not mean that other states intent on developing and deploying such capabilities—including Iran but also North Korea and others—should be allowed to do so without restraints or consequences. In late 2003, France, Germany, and Great Britain sought to deny, or at least stall, Iran's quest for nuclear status. Their EU partners followed soon afterward, thereby making it an EU initiative that was belatedly endorsed in the United States, where the allies' initiative had been initially questioned. Were these echoes of Bosnia twelve years earlier, when Europe's time was said to have come? In Iran, however, Europe's initiative does not depend on unavailable military capabilities in the face of an adversary determined to go to war to achieve his objectives, as was the case when the EU attempted to confront Serbia on its own; now instead, the EU initiative can rely on nonmilitary assets available to EU members, including the enforcement of sanctions that would be organized through the UN Security Council if Iran refuses to comply. EU failure to pursue the Iranian nuclear issue with some urgency might soon threaten to invite preemptive or even parallel military actions by any number of states, including the United States but also Israel, by a given date (namely an ill-defined point of no return after which Iran would have achieved nuclear self-sufficiency). For all intents and purposes, the danger raised by Iran to the cohesion of the alliance, not to mention the stability of the entire region, is greater in early 2005 than was the case with Iraq three years earlier. For Europe to assume otherwise would be the highest of follies: because the prospect of a nuclear Iran suggests an explicitly unacceptable endgame, Iran looms like a slow moving, multiple-fuse Cuban missile crisis, meaning the denial of an unacceptable outcome within a finite period of time.

Admittedly, there are in Iran many known unknowns—easily as many as there were about Iraq in the spring of 2002. But any debate about those ought to be based on two widely acknowledged premises—which is more than was the case with regard to Iraq on the eve of war.[6] First, an agreement with Iran must be reached before its nuclear capabilities are, or threaten to become, operational. Missing that time, or coming too close to it, would provide Iran with a nuclear shield that would complicate seriously any external attempt to moderate the more revolutionary aspects of its foreign policy in the region.[7] Second, while a military option will remain a plausible part of future negotiations, its scope as well as its duration would invite chaotic and potential catastrophic reactions. Intervention in Iran would not be about regime change, as for Iraq. But that is the least of the more significant differences: in Iraq, the people were not willing to fight for that regime, however willing (though not truly capable) they were to fight for their country; in Iran, people are both willing and able to fight for both, their regime and their country.

In short, Iran is a test that the EU must address, with active U.S. support; Afghanistan is a test NATO must pass, with more contributions from the EU; and Iraq is a test America cannot fail, with added contributions from both NATO and the EU. In all instances, these are immediate tests of global efficacy for the West and its institutions, but the efficacy thereby asserted will also determine the directions that America and Europe are most likely to pursue in the future—with, without, or even against each other.

On the eve of such tests, the United States and the states of Europe are more divided than at any time since the crisis that erupted over the rearmament of West Germany in the early 1950s, and the related calls for an "agonizing reappraisal" of the then-emerging ties between the two sides of the Atlantic. These divisions are not only bilateral—not even with France, America's most persistent challenger since June 1944, but also America's most troublesome critic since January 2002. Nor are they just personal—not even over George W. Bush, Europe's least liked U.S. president since Ronald W. Reagan in January 1981, but also Europe's most intrusive leader since Woodrow Wilson. Nor, finally, are these divisions circumstantial—not even over Iraq, admittedly the most significant cause for transatlantic discord since the end of the first Gulf War in February 1991. Instead, divisions between America and Europe reflect a structural crisis modified, to be sure, by personal, bilateral, and circumstantial tensions, but fundamentally rooted in the three major systemic changes of the past sixty years: the rise of American power to imperial preponderance, as a matter of fact, if not one of intent; the emergence of Europe as a reconstituted power in the world, notwithstanding its lack of military capabilities; and the transformation of the global security order since the horrific events of September 11, 2001, in the United States.

Reshaping that structure in order to preserve America's most complete relationship in the world will be neither quick nor easy, even though, as noted above, the agenda in and beyond 2005 promises to be urgent and daunting. The central issue is not about America's power and Europe's weakness, as it has become fashionable to argue in recent years, but about power and order, as it was argued in earlier postwar years. To this end, a credible commitment on both sides of the Atlantic to the renewal of their partnership is urgently needed, lest they both be faced with further tensions that could have been avoided otherwise. How well and how expeditiously America and Europe show their will for partnership during this second Bush administration will determine not only the terms of U.S.-European relations for the next generation but also the terms of the new world order during the first half of the twenty-first century. The moment is too urgent, and the partnership too vital, for America and Europe to pursue a self-defeating game of hide-and-seek that benefits neither and harms both. In 2005, it is for the United States to respond to Europe's need to be needed, not one country at a time but all of them simultaneously. But simultaneously, the states of Europe must also acknowledge that America wants its leadership to be wanted, not after it has worked but while it faces the challenging tests that stand in the way of goals shared across the Atlantic. To this effect, the will for a renewal of the Euro-Atlantic partnership rests on three principles:

First, the states of Europe and their Union must assume a larger role, commensurate with their new capabilities, interests, and influence. An unintended consequence of the war in Iraq was to bolster the image of Europe as an equal of the United States. Indeed, even in its current unfinished condition, the transformation of Europe stands as one of the major geopolitical achievements of the second half of the twentieth century, arguably one that is second to none. For the states of Europe to complete their Union remains a very important U.S. interest if only because it is a vital interest for the states of Europe. Admittedly, that view is not universally shared, and EU-phobic calls for a reappraisal of U.S. ties with the EU are no longer "agonizing" in the face of its alleged betrayal of America. In Europe, too, many deplore that transformation as a betrayal of each of its nation-states whose sovereignty was hijacked by the institutions they themselves created fifty years ago. That, however, is a flawed reading of the postwar logic of integration that recognized that the nation-states of Europe could not be rescued unless they were recast within the institutions that were launched accordingly.[8] These institutions, therefore, do not mark the end of European history but the end of a particular kind of history that midway in the past century was threatening to end Europe altogether, on behalf of one of its members or in the name of an ideology.

"Even if they did not actually create them, Europe's two twentieth-century wars revealed the forces that dominate the world today," wrote Raymond Aron early in the Cold War.[9] With a commitment of power to an institutional order that served its interests especially well, the United States helped control these forces in ways that gave birth to the New

Europe during the latter half of the past century. But in so doing, U.S. policies also unleashed new forces that are placing the world at risk during the first half of the new century. These forces threaten the security of all of our nations, as well as the safety of all their citizens. In 2005, as in 1949, the best way to control them is neither with an American nor with a European strategy, but with a Western strategy. Only to the extent that Europe and its Union contribute to that strategy—as an active counterpart welcomed by the United States rather than an adversarial counterweight that adds further obstacles—will it be confirmed that the transformation of Old Europe was not a betrayal of the U.S. idea of a strong and cohesive Euro-Atlantic West either.

For this to happen, however, Europe must avoid the internal divisions that deny it the voice it needs if it is to be heard on the basis of a power it can claim only if it is united. Four issues will be especially contentious during the coming four years, and may serve as benchmarks for how well the EU stays on course, and how effectively its alliance with the United States evolves and performs:

The two-year ratification debates for the EU constitutional treaty signed in October 2004 present risks for the EU but also for Europe's relations with the United States. With nearly half of the twenty-five members awaiting national referenda for ratification, the treaty is emerging as a bottom-up vote on EU membership. Although ratification by all is said to be required for the treaty to be adopted, rejection of the constitutional treaty by Britain would raise the prospect of a smaller "core" European Union led by France and Germany, which would move ahead toward the closer political union opposed by a smaller group of states led by Great Britain—an echo of the institutional conditions that existed when a small economic community was launched at the expense of the free trade area urged by Britain. How such a two-speed Europe would operate within a common European Economic Space is not clear—but how, and how well, a one-speed European Union will evolve, should the constitutional treaty be rejected by another large EU member like France, is equally unclear. Indeed, and source of further concern, constitutional referenda could also be turned into a bottom-up vote on Europe's will to form a closer Union as a counterweight to U.S. power and influence in and beyond Europe.

The future of the euro-zone, including the renegotiation and enforcement of the Stability and Pact Growth, is the second significant benchmark on the EU agenda. Europe is hardly near the write-off that is often claimed—with serious corporate restructuring finally getting under way, and Germany hoping for a long-awaited cyclical upturn. But the benefits of the single currency have not materialized as the big three euro-zone countries (France, Germany, and Italy) have lagged behind their smaller partners, and the three non-euro-zone countries (Denmark, Sweden, and, most of all, Great Britain) remained ahead of the EU while the full Union continued to be outperformed by the United States.[10] For a Union whose claim for power is legitimate only in its nonmilitary dimensions, the need to remain economically and institutionally strong is imperative lest its relevance to order be ended.

A third issue has to do with the performance of the new members, where there is an underlying public resentment over the form and pace of past negotiations for membership. In this context, the new EU budget for the years 2007–2013 is also a source of significant controversy among and within the members, especially at a time of painful cuts for most national budgets. Yet membership must have privileges—that is, recognizable benefits that outweigh the obligations it entails. The budget debate therefore raises the questions of institutional fairness, efficiency, and transparency that will shape the public commitment to membership—not only who gets what and how, but also who gives what and why.

Finally, a fourth issue has to do with new EU commitments for further enlargement, including especially Turkey (whose membership is unlikely to occur before 2013 even if negotiations were to start in 2005), not to mention the membership of Bulgaria and Romania by 2007, and possibly other decisions about Croatia and some Balkan states in 2010. Admittedly, Turkey's membership raises very serious internal issues for EU institutions that are yet to absorb the weight and the costs of their enlargement to the East. More immediately, however, with public opinion openly hesitant and often hostile to adopting an Islamic country that would further erode Europe's cultural identity, the consequences of such a decision on the constitutional debate cannot be overstated. Turkey's borders with Iran, Iraq, and Syria would open the door on delicate geopolitical issues and expose the Union further to the terrorist threats that might otherwise have been kept at a safer distance. Yet the continued exclusion of Turkey, or an overly extended negotiation for membership—let alone a sudden termination of these negotiations— would confine the EU to the "soft" functions that have defined it in the past, and deny its claims for the world power status to which it aspires for the future.[11]

Admittedly, the completion of the European Union—how, when, and with whom—is not a U.S. responsibility: it is the responsibility of its members. But because of the continued influence of U.S. policies, decisions that reinforce or weaken the fact or even the perception of the U.S. commitment to a united and stronger Europe will affect EU choices during the difficult period ahead—and, because of the growing influence of the EU, so will decisions that confirm or deny U.S. perceptions of an increasingly adversarial and dismissive Europe.

Second, a NATO that has gone global must be able and willing to act locally if it is to remain the security institution of choice for its members. During the Cold War, Europe's inability to produce more power was cause for exasperation but little else. After the Cold War, the limits of Europe's power were quickly exposed, as neither its leading nation-states nor their expanding Union were capable to assume the responsibilities they had claimed in Bosnia and elsewhere. Since September 2001, it has become clear that only a Euro-Atlantic partnership that relies on a better military balance can escape conditions that make a weak Europe look mostly like a dead weight relative to a powerful America whose preponderance makes it look like an imperial bully. Achieving such balance does not require America to become weaker or Europe to become as strong as America; more modestly, it demands that Europe itself acquire more of the military power it lacks so that America need not add to the power it already has.

Some in the United States are less sanguine about Europe's transformation to date. Instead, they point to the continuing crises of governance within its institutions and each of its members—to what has not been completed yet, or what fails to match U.S. standards, or what is threatened by trends said to be all the more irreversible as they confirm preconceived conclusions that Europe has already exceeded its "Eurotopian" potential as a global actor in world politics.[12] For these skeptics, the conclusion is self-evident: most of Europe is too old, too divided, and too compromised to be relevant; and in those few instances when it may be relevant, Europe is too hostile, too slow, and too weak to be helpful.

On the issue of capabilities, there is no need for subtlety. For the transformation of NATO to continue, and for the partnership to remain vital, Europe must gain additional military capabilities. With the exceptions of France and the United Kingdom, most European countries do not spend enough on defense: 2 percent of GNP should be a minimum, and fourteen European members of NATO did not meet that minimum in 2003.[13] To make matters worse, much of that spending is on personnel—about 60 percent—and little is left for procurement, leaving an estimated 80,000 troops (a mere 5 to 7 percent of the reported non-U.S. NATO troops in uniform) ready for deployment. For most European states, spending more and spending better is an obligation neglected for too long, and now too serious to be neglected much longer. Extending the accounting of defense spending to "soft power"—that is, to tools that permit to attract and persuade rather than to compel and coerce—is intellectually creative but it remains an alibi for continuing to spend less on defense than what is needed under current and predictable security conditions.

This condition creates a contradiction that is a significant source of current transatlantic tensions. As an unfinished union of states, Europe stands as a power in the world, with capabilities that are competitive in most dimensions of power except for military force, a saliency that is truly universal because of the reputation gained by its peaceful resurrection since 1945, and interests that are welcomed as a countervailing option to the United States. But lacking the political unity and military capabilities required for action when necessary, Europe is not, or not yet, the world power that it claims to be, and the price of consultation it demands is usually not worth the tangible benefits it brings.

Third, a comprehensive strategic compact is needed to develop a complementary approach to the post–Cold War, post-9/11 security agenda. This compact should aim at restoring an international legitimacy that America has been losing since the start of the war in Iraq. Indeed, for the first time since America assumed, on behalf of the West, a leadership it had earned the old-fashioned way, from Flanders in 1917 to Normandy in

1944, many of the European allies do not recognize the threat identified by the United States, do not condone the methods used to defeat that threat, and do not readily endorse the goals that motivate the U.S. role in the world.

Thus faced with a crisis of international legitimacy coming on top of a crisis of structural legitimacy, the United States and the states of Europe ought to agree on a strategic dialogue that would transform an alliance based on shared goals, overlapping interests, compatible values, and close intimacy, as it was developed for the Cold War, into the community of action that first became necessary after the Cold War but has become urgent since September 11. That, too, will not be easy. For the United States especially, but also for some of its senior European partners, a Euro-Atlantic community of action presupposes a willingness to give NATO a right of first refusal because of a natural predilection for NATO members as like-minded partners of choice. Yet, even assuming a broad strategic agreement on goals and interests, action that demands the use of military force cannot be managed by a committee of twenty-six NATO member states, including nineteen countries that also belong to another committee of twenty-five EU members, six of which are not NATO members.[14] That is a challenge to common sense. After the decision to act has been made by all NATO members, its enforcement should bear some resemblance to the contributions made by each ally, reflective of its willingness but also respectful of its relevance and cognizant of its capabilities.

As a second Bush administration gets under way, and after the historic enlargement of both NATO and the EU in the spring of 2004, new modalities in U.S.-EU-NATO relations are needed with the same urgency as was shown in 1949, when President Truman was starting a new presidential term after his surprising triumph over Governor Thomas Dewey. At the time, it took only a few months to sign a North Atlantic Treaty that revolutionized the nation's history, as well as the history of its relations with Europe. Not acting as urgently now would not only be a mistake, it would also be irresponsible.

Assuming a shared will for the Bush administration to take the tests of global efficacy with the European allies, and for the heads of state and government in Europe to face the tests of regional finality in cooperation with, rather than in spite of, their U.S. ally, the Euro-Atlantic partners need new institutional modalities of complementarity:

- European membership in NATO and the EU ought to converge, which is to say that all European members of NATO should aim at, and ultimately achieve, EU membership, including Turkey but also Norway (as well as Bulgaria and Romania), and all EU members should also aim at, and ultimately achieve, NATO membership, including Austria but also Sweden, Finland, and others.
- NATO and EU relations with countries that are not members of either institution ought to be coordinated, especially with regard to Russia. Territorial oddities like Kaliningrad, and institutional orphans like Ukraine, would also gain from such policy coordination, as would other countries that are not part of the Euro-Atlantic geographic area but are nonetheless seeking partnerships for peace and prosperity in its context—especially the countries of North Africa.
- Closer U.S.-EU relations are needed, and Europe's recognition of America's special status as a nonmember member state of the Union it helped to launch, but also as further U.S. acknowledgment of the EU as a partner of choice that deserves to be treated as the virtual state it has become relative to the nation-states that continue to control it. To this extent, the EU should invite the U.S. president to attend regularly the opening dinner of the semi-yearly EU summit, not in order to contribute actively to the decisions of the EU Council but in order to participate informally in the dialogue that precedes these discussions.
- Better coordination between NATO and the EU as two institutions whose parallel contributions to the war against global terror are indispensable if that war is going to be both won and ended. The future of a European security pillar is tied to NATO, and NATO's future is dependent on its ability to act globally—with capabilities enhanced by a better coordination of nonmilitary security tools between the allies, and a common understanding of the priorities they share on the basis of a more compatible strategic view of the world they face. At some early point in the future, this might best be achieved by giving the EU a right of attendance in the NATO Council, with comparable status for NATO at relevant EU meetings.

This is not a small agenda. But, as shall be seen in the pages that follow, it is not a new vision either—for it is in fact the vision that was articulated after World War II in the name of the Cold War, and now needs completion after the Cold War and in the name of the wars after September 11. Because there is a close and mutually reinforcing relationship between European integration and transatlantic cooperation, the need for finality encompasses both the EU and NATO with the goal of transforming a community of overlapping values, converging interests, and common goals into a community of complementary action. With the EU and around NATO, a comprehensive Western strategy will enable Americans and Europeans to do everything even if they do not do everything together. This challenge must be addressed by a renewed Bush administration and its counterparts in Canada and Europe with the same purpose and endurance as was shown when the transformation of Europe began fifty years ago, as a revolt against a failed past, a needed response to a dangerous present, and without a genuine understanding of an unpredictable future.

1

TEMPTATION
OF EMPIRE

The single events that will shape the next four years and, beyond George W. Bush, our future in subsequent years, are mostly unpredictable, but that need not be the case for their consequences too. To step out of the darkness that lies ahead, the past can serve as a convenient flashlight. Once in a while, however, the batteries run out: as the present loses its clarity, history itself appears to be at risk. "The very concept of history implies the scholar and the reader," observes George Kennan.[1] While the scholar helps preserve the authenticity of the past, the reader, too, is needed to maintain its relevance even when the wholeness of historical continuity is threatened by the apparent novelty of the moment. These, notes Hannah Arendt, are "moments of anticipation," which are "like the calm that settles after all hopes have died" but also, therefore, like the excitement that rises when new hopes are born.[2]

Early in the Cold War, the sight of falling empires in a powerless Europe was enough to foresee the collapse of the Soviet Empire. Believing it nonetheless unthinkable in later years sadly said more about the West than about its adversary. Why would the collapse of an evil regime and a fatally flawed ideology be deemed unthinkable until it had actually occurred? Still, after Moscow's imperial career had ended in the fall of 1991, American power reigned supreme. This, too, was a "moment of anticipation" when a new international order was forecast with enough confidence to announce an end to the essential continuity of history. Having successively defeated Nazi Germany, Imperial Japan, and Soviet Russia, the United States appeared to have defeated war itself. Who could have thought, then, that a decade later, the twenty-first century would open with unprecedented acts of violence against the nation's territory, soon followed by unfamiliar wars of regime changes in Afghanistan and Iraq? Who could have anticipated that on the eve of overtaking the tragic detours of history, America itself would be finally conquered by history?

August 1914, it can be readily agreed, was the defining year of the twentieth century—a "tragic and unnecessary conflict" that "destroyed the benevolent and optimistic culture of the European continent" and "left a legacy of political rancor and racial hatred so intense" that it conditioned all the events that followed.[3] Thus, a century that had opened as a good time to be alive unfolded instead as a century when it was a good time to die. Live or die, this was Europe's time. Before 1914, no foreign minister, sovereign, ambassador, and chancellor worried about the United States, none bothered to speculate on its strength, its attitude, and its participation in the impending conflict.[4] And yet, seemingly unbeknownst to the Great Powers of Europe, they were about to start a war they could not end on their own, thereby setting a pattern that defined the rest of the century. Europe died then, of course. But because it insisted on pretending otherwise in 1919—with victorious European states eager to impose their will on defeated states that remained bent on revenge—the Old World still faced the long agony of the interwar years. "What have we not seen, not suffered, not lived through?" wrote the Austrian humanist Stefan Zweig in 1943, in exile in Brazil where he had sought refuge from the world that had betrayed the values to which he had aspired.[5]

Significantly, after 1945 the major decisions for Europe were made by Americans who, however inexperienced they were with the burdens of global leadership, were acting at the invitation and with the approval of their European elders who understood that this was a final chance at redemption from their past sins and, eventually, at their countries' rebirth. Although many European "foreign ministers, sovereigns, ambassadors and chancellors" and lower-rank diplomats, intellectuals, and corporate leaders were involved with these decisions, this had ceased to be Europe's time and had become that of America. As we know now, this also proved to be a good time for all, Americans and Europeans. For where the wasted heroism of World War I had produced a peace to end all peaces, the dehumanizing brutality of World War II made it a war to end all wars—in Europe at least, where the decisions made then by the Truman administration—bold, generous, courageous, and ultimately visionary— helped Europe master its own past and start anew in ways that challenged the historian's own imagination.

While most would agree that September 2001 stands as an event of lasting historic significance for the United States, there still is little agreement on its actual meaning for the world. After that meaning has become clearer, what judgments will historians make of the decade that preceded September 2001—what was left undone and why, but also what should not have been done and why not? How will future historians assess the treatment of the defeated Cold War superpower, but also how will they judge the neglect of the countries at whose expense the other superpower had emerged victorious? Is it there—in and beyond Afghanistan—that will be unraveled the roots of the horrific attacks on the United States? Each of the global wars waged during the previous ninety years—now barely more than a lifetime—is still debated among scholars and between their readers. Will tomorrow's historians be distraught by what they uncover, like many are today when they reflect on the insanities of the First World War, the twenty-year descent to another round of collective murders during the Second World War, and forty years of relative indifference to the Soviet gulags and the ideological slavery of Eastern Europe? In sum, will September 11, 2001, be viewed as the brutal and vengeful awakening of earlier conflicts, or will that day merely be an aberration in an otherwise unaffected path toward a more orderly and just world rendered possible once again by American power?

That a withdrawal of U.S. power would make the future less promising and more dangerous should be especially convincing in Europe, arguably the main beneficiary of a global order defined on the strength of American power during the past century. Instead, doubts are mounting, as everywhere in Europe "foreign ministers, sovereigns, ambassadors, and chancellors" worry about America's preponderance. That any new order in the twenty-first century will be affected by the facts of U.S. power should not be in doubt. But now that Americans caught a glimpse of dangers that are too real and even urgent to be left to other countries or the institutions to which they belong, the temptation to make extensive use of that power may prove irresistible—together with others if possible and when useful, and without and in spite of others wherever and whenever desirable or necessary. Once again, Ulysses and Ajax are meeting in their never-ending Homeric odyssey—a struggle between wisdom and power, assuming that there can be enough of the former to guide the latter's quest for order.[6]

SIGHTS OF EMPIRE

In our time, the state of America's relations with its European allies responds to four interconnected facts. One is the collapse of the Soviet Union and the preponderance of American power, which the end of the Cold War finally left without any immediate competitor. Another fact is the integration of more and more countries in Europe as a European Union whose capabilities, interests, and influence already enable it to resist or support (but not deny) the sway of American power. A third fact is the impact of globalization, meaning "the abolition of distance and time" and, accordingly, the inability for any country, including the most powerful among them, to remain indifferent to developments elsewhere.[7] And the fourth fact is the unveiling of a new form of warlike terror, represented by, but not limited to, the events of September 11, 2001, when the "over there" of yesteryear's violence was brought "over here" in America.

These are facts. They are neither perceptions nor trends, even though their significance is affected by perceptions and conditioned by other trends. Nor are these facts myths, even though they can be readily distorted by the views that people hold about themselves and others—"our" past and "theirs," our intentions and capabilities relative to theirs. Nor, finally, can these facts, perceptions, trends, and myths be ignored. They are a constant part of the present because daily events remind us of their presence, strengthening our conclusions if not our resolve. September 11, 2001; November 8, 2002; March 17, 2003; March 11, 2004—history is weaving new trends around a calendar that reminds us of the ruins of the two towers in New York City, the collective will of UN Resolution 1441, the divisive war in Iraq, and the terror attack in Madrid—with much more to come. But these facts—perceptions, trends, and myths—

are also giving birth to a future that is feared because enough has already happened to feed our apprehensions about the risks of a new security normalcy that no one will escape because of its indivisible impact on all.

Waged in the context of these four interconnected facts, the war in Iraq confirmed earlier sightings of an American Empire—not only the war itself but also the debates that preceded the war and the U.S. decisions that shaped the outcome of those debates. The sight remains blurred, however. Absent the weapons of mass destruction used to justify preemptive military action in March 2003, the war was viewed by the critics of the Bush administration as a "war of choice" that was presented as a "just war" after Saddam's capture in December 2003. But by that time, failure to satisfy prewar expectations of a quick rehabilitation of the new Iraqi state and a related disengagement of the U.S.-led coalition forces had also exposed the limits of American power to end the war in the face of its allies' reluctance to help and its adversaries' resistance to concede. These limits are real and even significant, but they are not enough to make of the U.S. preponderance a short-lived occurrence—a so-called bubble.[8]

Is America an imperial power, and does she already control, or should she seek to acquire, an empire—and if so, what sort of empire and where? The reality of America's imperial power is a matter of facts: the United States is a state that exceeds others in capabilities, interests, saliency, and purpose.[9] It is not merely a great power: it is the greatest among them, a power that can unilaterally shape the behavior of others by means that include the threat or the outright use of force, as well as reliance on economic inducements, political dependence, and even personal ties or inspiration.[10] Having waged three global wars in the twentieth century, none of which it started and all of which it won, the United States now stands alone—a power without rivals and even without immediate challengers. Other countries in the world may defy it for a while but none can deny it for long, let alone coerce or defeat it. Its reach is awesome— "much more than the British Empire," wrote former French Foreign Minister Hubert Védrine, "and closer to what the Roman Empire was compared to the rest of the world . . . maybe not in terms of duration, but surely in terms of universality of influence."[11]

Americans are reluctant to claim such status, as a matter of principle as well as on grounds of intent. Proclaiming the imperial facts abroad is often enough to earn an anti-American label, as Védrine learned when his statements about the United States were given a hostile tone that he did not mean to give them. Historically, the accumulation of imperial power was sought actively and that quest in turn led to the acquisition of an empire, meaning the political control of weaker and often distant countries, directly or by proxy, occasionally for the better and usually for the worse—for the colonies at first but, soon enough, for the colonizing power as well. The imperial way is not the American way, however, and the only colonies America has known intimately are those that fought for their independence from the British Empire. Admittedly, from the time America was born it faced an imperial "destiny" that carried the republic "from sea to sea" and made it a potentially decisive force in the world.[12] But it never had the urge to expand much further beyond the Western Hemisphere. To this extent, it always was, and remains, an anti-imperial imperial power—so irreversibly so that it often was open to manipulation by the weaker states it was expected to dominate—"a virtual prisoner of its client states."[13] That is part of an imperial hubris that other imperial powers may have enjoyed, but which their people never believed as profoundly in the United States—thus giving Americans the ability to be what they are, but with the good conscience gained from knowing who they are not.

At home, in the United States, emphasis is placed on the more benign folklore of leadership and responsibilities. "You hold a coalition together by strong leadership," confided Condoleezza Rice on behalf of President Bush.[14] This is also the way in which President Truman's view of the nation's role in the world used to be justified. "The only way to lead is by leading," explained one of his main advisers shortly after the end of World War II. Even when the preponderance of U.S. power is acknowledged, subtle qualifiers provide America with a convenient alibi—an imperial power, yes, but one that is "adolescent,"[15] "compulsive,"[16] "benevolent,"[17] "oblivious,"[18] or "inadvertent,"[19] and even an "Empire Lite"[20] that emerged "by default" and is likely to be the "final" one of its kind.[21]

Such reluctance matters because it provides good reasons for a self-denial that is important on grounds of efficacy, as well as on grounds of durability. A strategy of preponderance that is in fact imperial requires a public will to endure the financial and human costs it demands. That is not to the liking of most Americans. "We should like an easy way to carry a heavy burden," observed Dean Rusk during the first serious postwar test of U.S. power in Korea, "an agreeable way to perform disagreeable tasks, a cheap way to bring about an expensive result."[22] The dream lives on. During the internal debates that preceded action in Iraq, the U.S. will to lead was not matched with a comparable willingness to tell the American people either the cost of the war to come or of the peace to achieve. Nor was there much ability to persuade other countries to follow. That, too, is an obstacle to the use of imperial power, especially as the executive branch of the U.S. government finds it easier to punish its foes than reward its allies and would-be friends, as most leading members of the coalition of the willing learned at their expense in Iraq. America lacks experience in this domain, as compared to European powers like France, which, during the war debate at the UN Security Council, found it easier to influence distant Cameroon than the United States could Mexico and Chile.

Being an imperial power is a full-time commitment that cannot be met in between elections and on the cheap. It is true that the temptation to use that power unilaterally can drive the imperial power out of the questionably safe institutional cage of multilateralism. For a country endowed with such preponderance, acting alone can produce significant gains relative to competitors that fail to follow and stay behind, while providing for economic and commercial benefits found in those places where control is asserted. The history of imperial powers, however, confirms that these advantages are usually exaggerated and generally not durable.[23] In any case, for a nation like America, which has most of everything, exploiting the resources of others is not necessary—as it was for Britain, for example—and for a people like Americans, access to distant lands is not especially appealing—the way Portuguese, for example, used to enjoy going to Angola. In short, America is the first imperial power that shows neither much interest in, nor a need for, an empire—meaning the imposition of its rule over distant lands and the forceful conversion of their subjects to the "good" things of the American life. Rather, it insists on the will to freedom and the peace that freedom brings as its distinctive credo—"beyond power, beyond interest, beyond interest defined as power."[24]

Yet, irrespective of intent, the facts of America's imperial power are convincing. Not only does it easily qualify on all accounts—capabilities, interests, saliency, and purpose—it surpasses most other countries on each account. The United States is more than the only superpower left after one hundred years of total wars all over the world. It is, in the words of Joseph Nye, the only complete power.[25] Even if the countries of Europe had the will, the know-how, and the resources required to challenge the United States, it would take two decades at least to make a dent on the current U.S. lead.[26] Nor is America likely to ignore a challenge to its predominance, irrespective of its source, as it did in the 1970s, when the rise of Soviet military power opened a "window of vulnerability." Indeed, the United States is now explicitly committed to extend, not just preserve, its superiority relative to any current or future rival that might stand in the way of its interests and values. Since September 2001, a surge in defense spending has confirmed America's ability to renew its power at will and after it had seemed to have already peaked. In 2003, defense spending exceeded the combined total of the next twenty-two largest military spenders; in 2004, it surpassed whatever the other 189 countries in the world spent. For now and the many years to come, there can be no military counterweight because there is no state or group of states with enough weight to near balance.

The U.S. preponderance is not limited to military power alone, however, even though it is not, admittedly, as compelling in other areas of power. Thus, the American economy surpasses that of its five closest national rivals combined—Japan, Germany, Great Britain, France, and China. During the latter part of the Cold War, Japan and Germany were widely viewed as America's main rivals. Since then, however, both economies have regressed or stagnated: Germany found it difficult to keep up with the EU, and Japan fell steadily behind China. As a whole, the EU was nearing economic parity after its first post–Cold War enlargement from twelve to fifteen members nearly a decade ago, but it has not met the promises associated with the single market in 1992 and the single currency in 1999. In 2000, gross domestic product per capita in the United States was nearly one-third higher than the EU average, and the gap has increased since.[27] Assuming zero growth for the American economy as of that date, Germany and Spain would still not catch up until 2015, while Italy, Portugal, and Sweden would have to wait until 2022.[28] Extrapolating from present trends, the U.S. economy may double the economy of an enlarged Europe within a generation—and projecting further into the future, demographic trends threaten to erode seriously the economic vitality of a Europe whose population is both aging and shrinking. In other words, even if an American Caesar was to be in need of a new Croesus, who accumulated vast wealth while Rome was busy expanding the reach of its empire, Europe may be unable to play that role by the time the need becomes truly apparent.[29] On such grounds, better turn to India or China, both of which at their worst still perform much better than Europe at its best.

Admittedly, warnings of a financial overstretch resulting from chronically unbalanced domestic finances are troubling. In the nineteenth century, the British Empire ran considerable current account surpluses that persisted until the outbreak of World War I. By comparison, the United States faces large deficits—which stood at 4.2 percent of gross domestic product even before September 11, and have moved near 6 percent since—and these deficits suggest an imperial premium that neither the United States nor the rest of the world can endure for long.[30] But that point has not come yet, and warnings of a financial overstretch are likely to be ignored by President Bush, as they were by President Ronald Reagan until he had built enough military surplus to win the Cold War without compromising an economic future that was booming within a very few years because of the very man-made nature of these deficits.[31]

The singularity of America's preponderant power does not end with the reluctance to build an empire of its own. America is also the first imperial power that is truly universal—more so than Rome or Alexander's Greece, and more convincingly than nineteenth-century Britain—because of the range of its interests, including an unprecedented belief in its values, and the reach of its saliency, including a widespread emulation of its institutions. At the start of the twentieth century, U.S. interests rarely went beyond the Western Hemisphere. Midway through the century, they centered on Europe, the original cradle of the American Republic. During the Cold War, when U.S. attention focused mainly on the Soviet Union, successive administrations remained sensitive to their allies' claims of imperial legacy—and hence, respected the primacy of France in West Africa or Southeast Asia, for example, or of Britain in Southern Africa or Southwest Asia. The imperial spread of American power was not planned.[32] It expanded wherever the fall of other powers took it, and whenever the rise of new powers threatened it. Now, however, U.S. interests leave little room for "improvisations" and even less time for "invitations." Rather, U.S. power goes wherever and whenever deemed necessary: to Iraq, Panama, Somalia, Haiti, Bosnia, Kosovo, Timor, the Philippines, Afghanistan, Iraq again, and Liberia, to cite but a few U.S. interventions since the end of the Cold War. Whatever is thought of America in the world, the world cannot escape America's reach. Whatever the risk of overextension there may be for the United States, countries abroad are increasingly concerned with an American temptation to impose its will and define the terms of change in the world at will. Indeed, whether the events of September 11 changed the world is moot: for America to assert that they did was enough for the world to be actually changed.

Few imperial powers in history have enjoyed as much saliency in the world as the United States. The American language is the language of choice for businessmen and diplomats, students and scholars, and others. Even Europe is entering the "final" phase of its institutional transformation with an implicit understanding that American (which used to be known as English) rather than French (which used to dominate even when Britain ruled) has become the common second language of the European Union. This is the language that all twenty-five European Commissioners initially named by President José Manuel Barroso in October 2004 claimed to speak, as compared to eleven of them who were still reported to speak French;[33] but more significantly, this is also the language that brings with it a populist culture that transcends its quintessential American identity and carries a lifestyle that undermines past national or even regional claims of U.S. exceptionalism. McDonald's is one symbol among many others—"the new version of America's star-spangled banner, whose . . . cultural hegemony ruins alimentary behavior" formerly viewed as a "sacred reflection" of national identity.[34] "I want to be like Mike," is no longer a credo for Americans only. The world wants to "be like Mike," even if most countries lack the athleticism, the confidence, and the discipline they need to make it a contest—meaning a lack of power, independence, and even institutions.

America never was a nation among others—a nation like any other; rather, it was born a great power—a nation like no other. From the beginning, it had the potential to assert itself against, and at the expense of, other world pow-ers, global or regional. But that potential remained mostly ignored outside the Western Hemisphere until the twentieth century, when Americans began to uncover the rights and privileges of power. The end of World War I was briefly an early temptation to become a power in the world, but neither the nation nor its leaders were prepared for America to become all it could be in the world. A second chance came after 1945, when the nation assumed a leadership role about which its people remained ambivalent and which their leaders did not fully explain. In 1961, President John F. Kennedy was, by his own account, ready to pay any price, bear any burden, and face any foe—and the American people showed enough confidence to follow at what was re-ported to be "the moment of greatest danger." But a premature death did not give Kennedy enough time, and civil unrest turned America's attention back to pressing domestic issues. In 1991, after the Soviet collapse, President George H. W. Bush had the capabilities to heed the imperial call after he had overwhelmed another inept and flawed regime during the first Gulf War. But Americans once again showed they would rather enjoy their well-earned peace dividends at home than spend them abroad. Only a decade later, in 2001, did events and personalities converge to confirm that the nation might at last be ready, intellectually and morally, to succumb to the imperial tempta-tion, meaning using power to pressure, intimidate, coerce, preempt, defeat, or bribe any state that could threaten or erode significant U.S. interests.

The imperial temptation is about whether to accumulate power and why, when to wield it and where, and how best to preserve it. This is a de-bate that began long before the wars in Iraq and Afghanistan or Septem-ber 2001, or the Soviet collapse a decade earlier, or even the start of the Cold War. It is a debate that is as old as the American Republic—over ab-solute moral judgments and the nation's responsibility to enforce them not only at home but everywhere else in the world. For the most part, the foreign policy architects of the Cold War prudently recognized the limits of the nation's power relative to its unlimited urge for justice. After these limits had been tested in Southeast Asia, they seemed to embrace a Eu-ropean mindset that emphasized a world order based on stability, bal-ance, and compromises. That approach produced a nation said to be on the decline, torn by the sad spectacle of defeat in Vietnam, humiliation in Iran, confusion in Afghanistan—and growing restlessness at home. By exposing anew the abuses of the evil regime against which the United States was waging war, the foreign policy architects of the 1980s surprisingly followed President Jimmy Carter's example and relied on the primacy of American virtue to restore the power that ended the Cold War and kept it ready to use with a zeal that was applauded after the U.S. was attacked on September 11, 2001.[35]

Unlike earlier years when America was defined by a will to do less rather than more, the new mandarins who managed the aftermath of September 11 showed a will to do more rather than less, even while the rest of the world appeared to fear the risks of America doing too much rather than not enough. This new breed of the "best and brightest" who populate the corridors of power every generation or so were capable and experienced—for the most part, people of convictions who had already lived most or all of their ambitions. As had been the case with their predecessors, their intentions were honorable and compelling—no less than to humanize and civilize a world that threatened to go mad after it had shown an enticing tendency to get better. But in the pursuit of their goals, the new mandarins were dangerously arrogant, predictably stubborn, openly dogmatic, and disturbingly unable to acknowledge, let alone adjust to, failure. They knew what they had lived, and showed little interest in learning anything else unless it confirmed what they already knew. It is as if the horrific events of September 11 and they had been waiting for each other[36]—a peculiar congeniality between an attack that could not be imagined and a war that was eagerly awaited. More than the decision to go to war, the mismanagement of postwar conditions in Iraq was the by-product of this encounter.

SOUNDS OF WAR

Sounds of war are never melodious. Other sounds from friends, adversaries, and bystanders distort what the principals mean to tell their various audiences. Abroad as well as at home, threats are heard as if they were meant to reassure, and reassurances are heard as if they were meant to threaten. Even as prospects for war grow, arguments to dismiss the threat that calls for the use of force or, assuming the threat, to deny its urgency, seem to gain in credibility. Other priorities are said to have first call on scarce or at least limited resources. "Appeasement" is not merely an option[37]—it is initially the option of choice for many who respond to a logic that is lived convincingly from one step to the next but makes little sense later, when historians wonder how so many clues could have been missed before action was finally taken. The temptation of empire rises in response to the urge for appeasement. It is a refusal to be timid—what others prefer to call prudent; it is oblivious to risks of miscalculations and failure—what others prefer to call arrogant; and it is intent on remaining consistent—what others prefer to call simplistic.

"When you look at contingencies," warned Paul Wolfowitz in the early 1980s, "you don't focus only on the likelihood of the contingency but also on the severity of its consequences."[38] That may well be a useful tool of analysis but it is not a recommended recipe for action: when considering action, it is not enough to focus on the unknown consequences of inaction because it is imperative to examine also the unintended consequences of action, whether successful or not. In any case, contingencies have a life of their own—from the moment they emerge to the moment they pass away. Most of them are known much ahead of time, but few of them are addressed before their time. That Wolfowitz was worrying about a takeover of oil fields in the Persian Gulf by a country other than the Soviet Union long before Iraqi forces moved across Kuwait and near Saudi Arabia is a case in point. Even when the threat and its source are readily identifiable, where and when to confront them is usually as unpredictable as how. Lacking sufficient clarity, the will for appeasement is neither an attitude nor a policy but it is part of a process that shows a distinctive cadence that moves from stark indifference to mounting panic: what is the threat about, why address it now rather than later, what else takes priority, how to proceed and with whom, and why not simply let it go or leave it to others to act? Whether relative to Germany in the 1930s, to the USSR for much of the Cold War, to Iraq in the 1990s, or to North Korea and Iran now, the process repeats itself even as the principals keep changing. The end point, however, is not always tragic. There are instances when confronting the would-be aggressor earlier might have made war come earlier too, and there is no guarantee that an earlier war would have been easier than a war fought later. In short, the question is not whether to appease but when to stop appeasing—when, that is, waiting any longer would be even riskier than taking immediate military action. In short, the need to remain safe tests the willingness to be wrong.

The culture of appeasement began to take hold of Europe after 1919.[39] Indeed, twenty years later, few Europeans were willing to fight, except for the Germans who were unanimously hostile to the treaty that had been imposed upon them at the close of World War I. With no European democracy waging the entire war except for Britain, this was not Europe's "finest hour." After 1945, and over the course of the Cold War, the sounds of war grew increasingly distant for people whose affluent lives mattered too much to be interrupted, let alone ended, in some foreign land or for reasons that would be forgotten as soon as the killing had ended. It is especially during and after the Vietnam War that large numbers of Americans, too, came to share that culture. In July 2004, that was the paradox of the doctrine articulated by presidential candidate John F. Kerry, as he pledged to "bring back this nation's time-honored tradition: The United States of America never goes to war because we want to; we only go to war because we have to." While assuming that he was making a case for the legitimacy of war, Kerry was in fact asserting a "standard" that made an open-ended case for the legitimacy of appeasement as few of the wars waged in the twentieth century could be viewed as wars that were waged because "we had to," with only two unequivocal exceptions—in World War II and in Afghanistan.[40]

The different consequences that the use of force may have in facilitating or preventing catastrophic outcomes can be shown with examples lived forty years apart, in 1922 and 1962, and forty years before the 2002 debate over war in Iraq.

As in 2002 relative to the Gulf War that had been waged in 1991, there was in 1922 much serious unfinished security business inherited from World War I. At the time, the target of the allies' discontent was a German state that denied the reality of its military defeat. According to the victorious states, Germany now needed to pay up and provide for the reparations imposed by the treaty its government had signed at Versailles in 1919. Otherwise, the French especially insisted that new Western sanctions be imposed by a "league" of nations that had held Germany responsible for the atrocities of the previous war. Germany's defeat was, predictably, the decisive proof of its guilt. While many Germans might acknowledge that they had lost the war, whether on the battlefield or at home, few were willing to agree that they had started it.

It is in this context that in the closing months of 1922, French President Raymond Poincaré was to demand vengeance on, and security against, his country's old enemy—"regardless of the damage his onslaught might inflict on the fledgling German republic." At issue was Germany's commitment to disarm, especially in light of the nonratification of France's mutual assistance pact with Britain and the United States, but at issue, too, was Germany's capacity to pay the exorbitant war reparations that had been negotiated in London the year before. On both accounts, the French were significantly more adamant than their main wartime allies—especially Britain, but also the United States, whose insistence on an expeditious repayment of its war loans made France and others all the more insistent on the payment of reparations. In the fall of 1922, these differences prompted a debate over Germany at the League of Nations, within each of the main European capitals, and even with the United States (though not a member of the League) from which there was to be no recovery either for the wartime alliance or for the postwar international organization. While London rose angrily against "the inherent perfidy and insincerity of French policy," as then-Foreign Secretary Lord Curzon put it,[41] the French raged against the impotence of the League where fruitless meetings had confirmed the League's fatal irrelevance three years after adoption of its Covenant.[42] To bypass the League, the French organized a small coalition of the willing—as it would now be called—with Italy and Belgium, to invade the Ruhr and end Germany's "formidable danger" to France and its allies.[43] Although Britain did not dispute Poincaré's aims, whether with regard to disarmament or with regard to reparations, the British government rejected the French method. So did the United States where a moribund Woodrow Wilson had reportedly wished "he could tell the French ambassador to his face that he would like to see Germany clean up" his country.[44] In fact, as we now know, the French invasion proved to be a monumental strategic error— perhaps the worst error made by a Great Power in the twentieth century until, allegedly, the errors of judgment attributed to President Bush for failing to anticipate the consequences of the U.S. intervention in Iraq eighty years later. In any case, the French invasion of the Ruhr, and the two-year occupation that followed, ended any remaining hopes for a moderate German government, as well as any prospect that a matured League of Nations could ever assume an effective peacekeeping role in and beyond Europe. For all purposes, that marked the end of the postwar years and the beginning of the interwar years: for by then, in the spring of 1923, another war with Germany was all the more unavoidable as there was no alliance in place to prevent it.[45]

Forty years later, in 1962, a global war looked once again possible a continent away, in the Caribbean, where the Soviet Union sought to deploy most of its medium-range ballistic missiles. Clearly, this was an existential issue for the United States but also for its allies, whose indifference to Cuba could not spare them the consequences of a war should Washington and Moscow come to that.

Even with hindsight, the lack of U.S. consultation with Europe during the first week of the crisis is surprising. For days, the Kennedy administration discussed issues of life and death for Europe in utmost secrecy. Throughout, Secretary of State Dean Rusk emphatically spoke of the "very great danger" the administration's "far-reaching decisions" would have on the NATO countries.[46] According to then Vice President Lyndon Johnson, "not to confer with them" was "a breach of faith"—but that did not seem to concern President Kennedy who did not find it of "much use consulting with" the allies, even the British, who would "just object" anyway. "Probably ought to tell them, though," concluded Kennedy subsequently, but only "the night before" making final decisions.

Admittedly, the availability of superior military force, coupled with a forceful leadership, helped Kennedy to achieve his goals while avoiding the war he seemed prepared to fight at whatever costs. But Kennedy had a strong hand in the Caribbean. The facts that defined the threat were not in question—if anything, the facts were understated—and the dangers it raised were clear and immediately acknowledged. The Soviet violation of an implicit rule of engagement with the United States was blatant, and its inadmissibility was not questioned at home or by the allies. Unless the threat raised by the Soviet deployment was eliminated, and respect of the U.S. influence in that region restored, anarchy would prevail, especially as the U.S. vulnerability to Soviet attack would be compounded by a misreading of the nation's will to fight, even in its backyard and on behalf of vital security interests.

In the fall of 1962, the debate at the United Nations was somewhat staged since Kennedy's decisions were being made outside its context. But the significance of the issue was not cause for debate, and the allies were fully supportive of a U.S. decision to which they knew they could not object in any case. Even though they feared the consequences of a U.S. decision to use force, there was no serious attempt to block it. Indeed, the allies' confidence in the United States during the crisis was also a show of confidence in the U.S. leaders who managed it. There were no calls, for example, for Dean Rusk to assert more control relative to the U.S. president—as was the case in late 2002, on behalf of then Secretary of State Colin Powell and at the expense of the president he served. Nor was there any need for evidence that would confirm America's concerns after these had been communicated to its allies. "I accept what you tell me," de Gaulle told Kennedy's emissary grandly, "as a fact, without any proof of any sort needed."[47] The unintended consequences of the crisis came later: when some of the allies, especially France, reacted to the lack of consultation during the first, formative week of the crisis, by seeking more autonomy from the United States outside NATO; and when the Soviets reacted to their military inferiority with a strategic buildup that brought them close to military superiority while moving them even closer to economic exhaustion. But Kennedy's prudent handling of the crisis also helped avoid war, not only then and in the Caribbean but also anywhere else later. Indeed, notwithstanding occasional brinksmanship from either side, never again was there a confrontation that might seriously be viewed as conducive to a general war.

In September 2002, the new national security strategy trumpeted by the Bush administration pledged "to act preemptively" before "rogue states and their terrorist clients . . . are able to threaten or use weapons of mass destruction against the United States and our allies and friends."[48] In so doing, the Bush administration viewed the "thirteen-day crisis" as a model, or at least a precedent, for its policy in the Gulf region. Yet the 1922 debate at the League of Nations, and what is known of its aftermath, might have been a better analogy, not only because of the issues raised during the debate but also because of the risks assumed when the decision to use force was made in opposition to the will of the League. Like the French government in 1922, the Bush administration was exasperated by the ineffectiveness of an international organization that raised obstacles to the resolution of the urgent security questions inherited from the previous war. Like France in 1922, the United States made a last-minute effort to involve the United Nations and its leading members, but also like France, the United States proved unable to convince its interlocutors of the imminence of the threat raised by the previously defeated state. Like France in 1922, the security issue raised by a known enemy was deemed existential, and in both cases the decision to use force preceded the debate that followed with a passion also justified in both cases by the fact that none of the participants could escape the consequences of that decision. And as proved to be the case after the French invasion in 1923, the U.S. invasion of Iraq in 2003 might ultimately emerge as a colossal error if it were to end in a failure that had been feared by all but envisioned only by a few.

COUNTERWEIGHT AND COUNTERPART

Iraq was a European failure before it became America's failure.[49] That failure had to do with Europe's inability to construct a coherent multilateral framework for the post-9/11 security normalcy, which the United States would join because of what its European allies could contribute and achieve, rather than one that America could ignore because of what its allies would otherwise disrupt and might even deny. During the Cold War, tensions resulting from these conditions of Atlantic pluralism always were an inherent dimension of the Alliance, but they were usually mitigated by Europe's dependence on the United States for security—with emancipation from U.S. domination hardly a good idea when faced with the prospects of the Soviet subjugation that might follow.[50] However risky U.S. domination was, its alternative was always deemed to be worse. Even after the Cold War, the European allies' reactions to the growing superiority of U.S. power was moderated by the residual benefits of the security guarantee they continued to receive from their senior partner, especially as Europe remained unwilling to achieve world power status with more political unity, greater defense expenditures, and a renewed commitment to using force as and where needed. But after September 2001, these tensions ceased to be primarily European choices and focused instead on an American refusal to allow a number of European governments to make George W. Bush and his alleged imperial intent the central issue, instead of Iraq or Saddam and his reported stockpile of weapons of mass destruction. Accordingly, in 2002, the transatlantic and intra-European debate over Iraq was a debate over the uses of American power—where and when, how and why. Even more broadly, the debate had to do with the nature of global order and how best to regulate it: with competitive counterweights aimed at the restoration of a multipolar world in which the U.S. preponderance would be somehow balanced; or with reciprocal counterparts that would enable all members of the alliance to influence each other, help each other, and moderate each other.

At a first glance, the ideas of counterweights and counterparts are mutually exclusive. A counterweight suggests opposition, because of conflicting interests or even for its own sake. By comparison, counterparts call for cooperation, because of interests that are compatible, overlapping, or shared, and because they can be best enhanced with policies that are common or at least complementary. In practice, however, both ideas converge. For one, they both demand capabilities that give the designated or aspiring counterparts the weight needed to complete and even, on occasion, redirect what the preponderant partner does or can do. These tasks parallel those a counterweight would be expected to pursue, but they need not be carried out in an adversarial manner, depending on the broader relationship between the countries involved.

Looking ahead, Europe may not be able to gain sufficient power to ever become a credible counterweight, and assuming it can, a stronger Europe may not be willing to play its role with, rather than separately from, the United States. During the Cold War, only the threat "they" raised in the East defined the alliance "we" formed in the West. Thus, while the Soviet Union and its ideology explained what the alliance was against, they failed to define what it was for, especially outside the collective defense community where the alliance always seemed in crisis. Under such conditions, taking seriously the idea of a united Euro-Atlantic community, including an ever closer Union and an ever more powerful America within an ever more vital alliance was never easy. In the United States, NATO was widely seen as the main expression of the West, and the rise of European institutions was an afterthought inspired by American history, nurtured by American policies, and guaranteed by American power embedded in NATO. At no time was there much lasting concern that a united Europe could ever turn into a counterweight, except possibly over trade; most of the time instead, there was much disappointment over the recurring evidence that a Europe that always fell short of expectations was bound to remain a counterfeit, especially over security. In other words, even a progressively stronger (but hopelessly weak) Europe was understood as a passive counterpart of the United States—a noncontributing follower of U.S. leadership—as a matter of fact since it lacked the capabilities to do more, as well as a matter of intent since it lacked the will to do better. It is true that from the start this condition was due to an explicit threat that was too powerful to be countered alone, and thus left half of the European continent at the mercy of America's goodwill for protection against the other half. But over time, Europe's dependence also came to be resented as an implicit U.S. goal that might have been inadvertent after 1945 but now seemed welcome even if the immediate threat from the Soviet Union was to recede and "as the ante to ensure a central place for the United States as a player in European politics."[51]

Nor was Europe's resistance to U.S. leadership ever decisive during the Cold War. To this day, it is difficult to point to any significant U.S. policy that was derailed by the opposition of an ally in Europe—comparable, say, to what occurred during the 1956 Suez crisis when even jointly neither Britain nor France could act effectively in the face of U.S. opposition. At most, the timing of some U.S. policies occasionally suffered, as was the case with Germany's rearmament in the early 1950s, or with the deployment of intermediate nuclear forces (INF) in the early 1980s. Initiatives like the Multilateral Force (MLF) in 1963, or the Year of Europe, ten years later, primarily aimed at preventing Europe from doing what some in the United States did not want its European allies to do rather than at doing what some in Europe wanted the United States to do. In other words, these initiatives aimed at political goals—including, most of all, France's diplomatic isolation in Europe—that had been broadly satisfied by the time President Lyndon Johnson abandoned the MLF and President Richard Nixon forgot about the Year of Europe.

Limited, too, were the prospects of Europe's rise as a complete power, including military power. This latter dimension was always viewed as Europe's endgame. As George Kennan put it shortly after World War II, and long before the process of European integration had gained momentum, "Military union should not be the starting point. It should flow from the political, economic, and spiritual union—not vice versa."[52] But Europe's goal was never to "counter" American power in some illusive multipolar world—which is in the end the reason why the idea of a European third force never gained much momentum in the early 1950s, but also why de Gaulle never considered a withdrawal from the alliance after he took France out of NATO in 1966.

Americans who rejoiced over Europe's progress in the "economic and [the] spiritual" areas questioned its potential in the political and military areas, where initiatives announced in the name of Europe often looked like alibis for the nation-states to do little of what America wanted and less than what they claimed. In September 1950, the Truman administration viewed the French offer of a European Defense Community (EDC) as a "politically impossible and militarily unfeasible subterfuge" designed to avoid or at least postpone the U.S. calls for Germany's rearmament.[53] As events came to show, such skepticism was warranted, and even if the EDC was not so designed, the ideas behind the French proposal were too extravagant to be feasible, thus making it politically doomed from the moment it was put forward. Still, if anything, the EDC taught that for any European defense and security community to be viable, Britain's participation was needed from the start. A decade later, a French attempt to form a new bilateral security relationship with Britain was, therefore, the basis for another French attempt to make Europe less dependent on U.S. power. But that goal was known to be distant—"in fifty years," Charles de Gaulle told Prime Minister Harold Macmillan in December 1962.[54] This was the time needed, according to the French president, because "the Europeans must be on par with the Americans. That is my dream and if we don't achieve it now, no one will achieve it after us." In return for Anglo-French defense cooperation, de Gaulle would approve London's agonizing bid for membership in the Common Market (a late bid encouraged by the Kennedy administration). But expectations of a deal floundered a few weeks later, when President Kennedy convinced the British prime minister that his country's future still stood across the Atlantic with the United States and NATO, rather than across the English Channel with France and the EC. "There is a perception," noted Prime Minister Tony Blair in Warsaw in October 2000 that "de Gaulle was anti-British. . . . Nothing could be more misguided. . . . [He merely] saw Britain as both a Trojan Horse for the United States and a brake on the necessary strengthening of Europe."[55]

The French interest in multipolarity was revived after the Cold War and was gaining much traction before September 2001. "Working for a better organization of the international system in the 21st century," observed President Jacques Chirac in late 1999, "implies first of all moving toward a multipolar world."[56] Maybe encouraged by the discussions he had had with Tony Blair in St. Malo earlier that year, the French president declared "a balanced dialogue among regional poles" to be "in everyone's interest," especially as it could exist, *noblesse oblige*, "only if the European Union itself becomes a major pole of international equilibrium."

There is much that can be debated in Chirac's analysis, but there is also plenty to question in the rebuttals it has occasioned. It is "troubling," said Condoleezza Rice in late June 2003, that "some [in Europe] have spoken admiringly—almost nostalgically—of 'multipolarity,' as if it were a good thing, to be desired for its own sake."[57] But why fear it, as if being and remaining the only pole of power in the world is a goal that justifies any burden and every commitment? Why evoke it, to paraphrase Rice, "as if it were a *bad* thing, to be *opposed* for its own sake?" Beyond everything else that has already been mentioned—capacities, saliency, interests, and purpose—answering the imperial call demands durability, which must be acknowledged by the subjects but must also be tolerated by would-be challengers. That is not the forte of the American people, that is not common practice in the world, and "balanced dialogues" with other regional poles would help to reinforce the U.S. pole wherever its power might fail to relate and whenever its patience might fail to endure. Power moves, and unipolarity can only last a moment: ascending powers and new coalitions between them will see to it. In due time, but not too far from now, America and Europe will be more concerned with Asia than with each other, and they may be more concerned with the role of China in the Greater Middle East than with that of Iran or any reported Islamist state. For those who urged a balanced Euro-Atlantic dialogue in 2003, the case became subsequently stronger when growing insecurity in Iraq confirmed that the small coalition of the willing organized to wage the war in Iraq was not sufficiently capable to end it, in that country and within the region. In short, multipolarity is not a code word aimed at toppling America's imperial power but it is a key word to define the new world order that looms ahead. As Chirac put it in early 2004, "*ce n'est pas du* wishful."[58] After the Cold War, more Europe need not mean less America, just as during the Cold War more America hardly came to mean less Europe.

"Americans," de Gaulle said in September 1966, in his inimitable style, "are Englishmen who decided to live their lives when they grew up. But they remain brothers."[59] Today, the description offered by a European about America might be attributed to an American speaking of Europe writ large—as a continent, a union that chose to live its life after it became united; "but they remain brothers." Isn't that what then-French Foreign Minister Dominique de Villepin implied in late August 2003, when he insisted that "the French vision of multipolarity does not aim in any way to organize rivalries or competition, but rather responsibilities, stability, and initiatives."[60] In defense of American policies, as these have successfully evolved over the past one hundred years, but also in defense of European policies, as these have made it possible for Europe to be successfully transformed over the past fifty years, there is no reason why a multipolar world, an inevitable part of the future, cannot be organized more effectively and more lastingly with more cooperation between an American pole liberated from its imperial temptation and a European pole freed of its provocative instincts, both with a different mix of power and weaknesses and accordingly complementary in their action.

2

A CRITICAL JUNCTURE

M emories of the Cold War spring from the visionary decisions made by President Truman after World War II. Predictably, these decisions were applauded after the policies they helped launch worked. Yet, a certain air of destiny had quickly spread as the senior members of the Truman administration grappled with the historic significance of their postwar moment: "to create half a world," wrote Dean Acheson afterward, "a free half."[1]

The juncture was critical. Rooted in the nation's history, America's instinct was to come and stay home, now that the war was "over, over there." Prior to 1945, the United States had never felt comfortable abroad, except on its own terms—which other countries had not felt comfortable with either. Still, after Americans had been exposed to the dangerous ways of the world twice in slightly more than a generation, they seemed better prepared to embrace a grand strategy whose open-ended rhetoric belied the limited nature of U.S. ambitions. Nearly sixty years after the fact, we know now that the moment faced during these critical years was a defining moment—a moment, that is, during which the decisions that were made, and how, as well as the ways in which these decisions were enforced, and with whom, proved to be of lasting consequence for all.

In this defining moment, the United States was especially sensitive to the chaos left by the defeated states in Europe and, to a lesser extent, in Asia. Instinctively, the transformation of the Old World was perceived as the most significant and the most urgent geopolitical challenge to the world order that America hoped to construct. To this effect, the Truman administration made a series of bold decisions that were designed to reinvent peace in Europe. These were not always as coherent as historians have made them out to be, but they worked because they served a wide range of interests that were understood by, and were known to be at risk on, both sides of the Atlantic.

These decisions were cause for much public debate in Europe, and that is not surprising in light of the ambivalence that was shown at the time toward U.S. leadership; what is surprising, however, is that there was not as much debate in the United States, especially in light of the ambivalence that was widely felt about Europe. For what Truman engineered was a genuine revolution in American diplomacy. Now the U.S. role in the world would no longer be exerted from a distance and alone but close up and with willing allies, about which little was known except their potential for new disorders to which America could no longer remain indifferent. Yet whatever uncertainties Americans, too, felt about Truman, Europe, and the world, they had total confidence about their country's power, virtue, and values. It is that confidence that determined their faith in the country's ability to balance interests, commitments, and purposes. Notwithstanding the many setbacks and improvisations of the immediate postwar years, public questions about the Truman strategy therefore came only in later years, timidly during the Korean War but more loudly during the Vietnam War—when the costs of the nation's unintended rise to globalism came to be better understood.

On occasions, to be sure, there were prophetic warnings about the consequences of Truman's decisions. For theologian Reinhold Niebuhr, for example, "eminent proconsuls . . . partly drawn from the army and partly from business"[2] would ultimately engineer a new American Empire composed, added Walter Lippmann, "of disorganized, disunited, feeble, or disorderly nations, tribes, and factions."[3] But such concerns were on the whole ignored and isolationist pressures promptly overcome. Henry Wallace, whose presidential campaign in 1948 was largely based on his objections to Truman's foreign and security policies, received less than one million votes; four years later, Senator Robert Taft, a conservative republican who was wary of America's entangling commitments, failed to win his party's nomination, like General Douglas MacArthur who questioned the president's will to enforce his own rhetoric. Doing less than what Truman had said was no more an option than doing more than what Truman had already done. Admittedly, the United States was already a power without peers, able to build an empire of sort; but Truman entertained no such design, and had he shown any the public would have resisted it. In short, there was at the time neither an imperial temptation nor a need for empire. The American vision was not to expand the country out of its borders, but to make it possible for Americans to live safely within their country's borders. To this end, American power set out to create a pluralist West—a group of states that would not fear their diversity while they sought solidarity and even after they achieved unity.

Achieving this goal was not expected to be easy. Predictably, it would demand much time and even more restraint—two commodities known to be in short supply in the United States. To begin the world anew required first a reform of the European heartland, where war had become a way of life that had placed America at risk twice during the previous thirty-odd years. The U.S. intent was to bring more of America into Europe: to make Europe less European and more American—a political heresy that could only be entertained by a people that had lived safely at the margins of history and could, therefore, choose to ignore it. In short, America did not set out to extend its hegemonic control in and over Europe; that would have meant a single Western union of states in which the lesser partners would surrender their sovereignty and their identity to their former dependency across the Atlantic. Rather, America set out to help promote a new Europe, less divided and more peaceful, with which it could manage a more orderly Euro-Atlantic area. The vision was neither American nor European but both. For the West to be united as one, there had to be two distinct areas linked together as a Western community of states whose converging interests would rest on compatible values that might ultimately permit joint action.

THE SIGNIFICANCE OF THE PRESENT DEBATE

Once again, the end of a war, however "cold" it was, and the start of a new conflict, whether labeled a "war" or not, are testing the U.S. role in the world and, cause or effect, the history of U.S. relations with Europe. Once again, Americans debate the relevance of their alliance with like-minded European countries relative to other parts of the world. Once again, Americans and Europeans seem to be drifting away from each other as the Old World responds to an institutional discipline that imposes constraints that the New World has come to abhor under security conditions deemed to be immediately existential. There have been other such debates in the past: the recent history of America's relations with its allies is a history of discord behind which is hidden a record of remarkable achievements. But with the Cold War a full decade behind, and with many years of the war on terror looming ahead, the juncture has not been as critical since the postwar years. Not only is the enemy more elusive than ever before, allies and friends, too, are less recognizable than ever before. Learning to live without Europe is no longer said to be a risk but an opportunity that would unload "the most pernicious piece of Cold War baggage," namely "the stubborn Euro-centrism" of the U.S. role in, and strategy for, the world.[4]

This is paradoxical, to be sure. America's allies and friends should be most readily available in Europe, which defined not only the birth of America as a nation in the nineteenth century, but also the rise of America as a Great Power in the twentieth century. "People," wrote Samuel Huntington, "define themselves in terms of ancestry, religion, language, history, values, customs, and institutions."[5] That being the case, a Western identity can best be found within the shared structure that bridges the Atlantic divide, including the Atlantic Alliance and NATO. "Could not Americans and Europeans," asks Robert Kagan nonetheless, "simply say to one another, in the words of Bob Dylan, 'You go your way, and I'll go mine'?"[6]

Because comparable apprehensions were felt before, they can readily be ignored as a difficult but temporary moment of tension in transatlantic relations. In 1947, too, neither Americans nor Europeans fully agreed, among themselves as well as with each other, over the journey they were about to start—not only its end point but also the most effective ways to get there. In Europe, Truman's leadership was questioned—the man, as well as the country, both disturbingly provincial and dangerously miscast for their new roles. In the United States, even Truman lacked confidence as he did not count himself among the "few men in all history [who are] the equal of the man into whose shoes [he was] stepping"—not just because "the greatest of men had fallen" but because "the least of men—or at any rate the least likely of men—had assumed his place."[7] Truman now evokes more respect, of course. The ideas that shaped his sense of the postwar world, and the policies that helped to enforce these ideas after his election in November 1948, are widely considered as visionary—those of a man whose character and will made him destined for greatness. Then, however, these ideas and their author were often dismissed as naïve, and those decisions were questioned as dangerous. Rebuild and rearm Germany? Stay in and unite Europe? Contain the USSR, topple communism, and liberate Eastern Europe? Americans, it was feared in Europe, lacked the experience and the endurance needed to lead Europe, whose history they had not lived and thus failed to understand, and whose geography they had not known and thus failed to recognize. Europeans, it was countered in America, lacked the resilience and the pragmatism needed to refashion themselves and their continent as a united and stable whole.

These concerns were misplaced, and the Atlantic (and European) crises to which they gave birth periodically were always short lived. Yet, standing in the way of complacency are many features that make today's debate fundamentally different from earlier debates. So it is, for example, about its participants. Unlike what used to be the case, the most articulate and convincing skeptics are no longer questioning the success of American policies, especially in Europe and since World War II. To argue differently would make little sense in light of what is now known. Nor are there doubts over the fact that these policies served U.S. interests well: unprecedented affluence in, as well as security within, Europe has provided direct and substantial benefits for the United States. Because of these results, today's most credible critics are often convinced Atlanticists who have applauded and even contributed directly to developing and enforcing these policies. But instead of wishing to stay the course for a Euro-Atlantic finality that would spill over from Europe and its Union to the United States and its alliance with Europe, they are now openly weary of the conditions that lie ahead. They fear, in short, an intrinsic incompatibility between a changing America and a changed Europe, as the former shows little patience for the "global tests" that European countries hope to impose on U.S. leadership—no longer a passionate "family dispute" with irreversible commitments but a brutal strangers' fight over conflicting purposes.[8]

For the new breed of Euro-Atlantic skeptics, the imminent "end of the West" is forecast without satisfaction.[9] Such announcements bring their authors close to the unthinkable, which has to do with the risks of an ill-defined transatlantic divorce. They would much prefer another fate for the institutions that promoted peace and achieved prosperity after World War II—a different fate for America, left alone in an increasingly dangerous and hostile world. "The West is being lost," deplored French defense expert François Heisbourg in the spring of 2003, amidst the many "fault lines" that are "unmaking the alliance" especially as "U.S. hawks . . . [who are] simply not interested in the alliance" take precedence over those who continue to believe that "it is worth trying to rescue the transatlantic relationship."[10] One year later, America's "stubborn activism and unlimited incompetence" lead Heisbourg to "plead [though with "much sadness"] for the disassociation between Europe and U.S. policies that have become too hazardous under President Bush."[11] The same anxious tones are heard when the warnings—that the West is at risk, or that either side might be better off without the other—are issued in the United States by the very architects of the Cold War transatlantic order—like former Secretary of State George Shultz, as he wistfully reflects that "maybe we don't" need the Atlantic Alliance after all.[12]

Admittedly, such concerns have been heard before. But a generation ago, forecasts of the end of the alliance were mainly statements of failure. Europe, it was then said, had become an "American protectorate" that was "increasingly unviable" because "while still immensely powerful, the United States is nevertheless markedly weaker in relation to its own allies, the Soviets, and the rest of the world."[13] Indeed, the future envisioned for Europe in the mid-1960s was linked to a "new postwar world" that combined "the appeal of [French] Gaullism" relative to the United States, and the "passing of American omnipotence" relative to the Soviet Union.[14] That being the full measure of the skeptics' argument, a surge of Soviet hostility or a burst of U.S. leadership was enough to restore faith in the Alliance and order among the allies, even among the most committed critics of U.S. policies—up to de Gaulle himself.

By comparison, today's arguments are structural, centered as they are on the need for a renewed Europe to balance the U.S. preponderant power with a power Europe already has in most areas but lacks in the military area. Previously, the demise of the West was argued in terms of the deconstruction of America and the decline of its leadership, as a matter of will and as a matter of facts. Now it has to do with the reconstruction of Europe, including its enlargement to the east, the launch of a single currency, an ongoing reorganization of its institutions, and the ever elusive European Security and Defense Identity that would make it whole at last. But being the closest thing to an equal that the United States faces at the beginning of the twenty-first century is not the same as being close at all, especially in the military area.[15] Still, even in the absence of military power, have legitimate differences between the allies now become so large as to preclude common policies and encourage instead separate and even adversarial action? The question goes to the core of what an alliance is expected to do—namely, bring each state to do on behalf of its allies what it might otherwise have chosen to not do, and avoid doing, also because of its allies, what it might have otherwise elected to do.

Also novel is the immediacy that surrounds these arguments. The timeline for entering the future has been dramatically shortened. These are the "last days" of the alliance, and so they seem to remain as perpetually extended deadlines come and go. By the time the new NATO members are officially welcomed in 2004, it was written shortly before the war in Iraq, "NATO's lights will be flickering, leaving it up to the European Union to take command of Europe's security."[16] After the end of major combat operations, the forecast was refined by others, who somberly anticipated that "what the [Bush] administration trumpets as "victory" in the Persian Gulf may prove, in reality, to have pushed NATO into terminal decline, given the decisive boost to the political unification of Europe."[17] The more specific these forecasts, the more easily they are revised by their authors or amended by their adherents. Yet relative to past forecasts, these conclusions are paradoxically cause for some satisfaction as they implicitly celebrate the rise of the EU and, therefore, praise the U.S. leadership that established the broader Atlantic organization within which the EU proved to be possible. A strange and new breed of part-time neo-Atlanticists can thus find "love" for the EU on geopolitical rather than emotional or ideological grounds—"because in this messy world we're living in, two United States are better than one."[18]

America's discovery of a new Europe—bigger, more united, and stronger—is relatively recent. When rejecting Paul Kennedy's thesis of an irreversible "decline" of American power, Samuel Huntington viewed an ascending Europe as the only plausible challenger to American primacy. Only Europe, he surmised, had "the population resources, economic strength, technology, and actual and potential military strength to be the preeminent power of the 21st century."[19] Not the least visionary part of Huntington's forecast was that it anticipated the leaps about to be made by the European institutions after the Cold War, beginning with the Maastricht Treaty in December 1991. Unlike many of his followers, however, Huntington did not fear the impact of Europe's rise on U.S. interests but instead welcomed its contribution to U.S. power and Western influence. After the declinists' gloom of the early 1980s had been overtaken by events, other fashionable ideas soon emerged, including Francis Fukuyama's "end of history" followed by Huntington's own "clash of civilizations." But, even as the Cold War ended, Americans who acknowledged the reality of Europe's economic integration still viewed it as a dangerous political illusion that encouraged Europeans to attempt more than they wished, or could, deliver, including a challenge to the United States they could neither afford to mount nor even afford to win.

In the summer of 1995, Bosnia was a harsh awakening for Europeans who had believed that "the hour of Europe" had come. Americans, left with the evidence of Europe's insufficient military capabilities and political will, concluded that there could be no relief yet from the "burdens" assumed after World War II and throughout the Cold War. Yet, as President Clinton was about to leave office, neither the U.S. late intervention in Bosnia, nor the first NATO war in Kosovo or the first enlargement of the alliance in the East provided more than a widespread understanding that the United States still had to play a central role in post–Cold War, pre-EU Europe. What that role might or ought to be specifically was un-clear. Defining it was left, therefore, to the new administration whose neoconservative view of the nation's role in the world had been conceived during the Nixon-Ford-Carter decade of alleged decline and retreat, had grown during the Reagan years of renewal and rollback, had deepened during the bitter decade of Republican exile that followed in the 1990s, and had blossomed under the triumphant conditions of economic and military preponderance that prevailed in early 2001.

I LIKE YOU—NEITHER DO I

How are we to account for the bitter tone that characterized America's di-alogue with Europe—if that is what it was—after the emotional outburst of public support that followed the events of September 11, 2001, in the United States? Why is there such anger in America at its allies in Europe, and why are there such doubts in Europe about America? How to explain the ambivalence shown by most Europeans about the facts and intentions of American power on the eve of, and since, a military action aimed at a tyrannical Iraqi regime opposed by all (or almost)? Why is it that at the peak of its power, a vulnerable America is faced not only with the loss of its invincibility but also with an apparent decline of its relevance? Is it the values we cherish, the leaders we elect, the power we hold, or simply the friends we keep—is it merely who we are or what we do that is cause for so much polemic, and now widespread anger and even hatred?

These questions are not new but they are heard in the United States with considerable bitterness and growing resentment. We, it is claimed, deserve better. "Why," asks historian Walter Russell Mead, "with a record so active and glorious, is American foreign policy held in such low es-teem?"[20] The question is appropriate, but it can be carried to an extreme. Europeans whose transformation responded to a U.S. leadership that helped to overcome their worst instincts need a few lessons in history—reminders not only of what they used to be, but what they have become and how. For the results attributable to such leadership are, or should be, convincing: while Europe's tragedies of miscalculations and defeats un-folded in America's absence during the first half of the twentieth century, its more recent history of renewal and redemption has unfolded in America's presence. What is surprising, therefore, is that instead of causing satisfaction in the United States, a new Europe that no longer equates the nation's fiber with its people's enthusiasm for wholesale killing is evoked in the United States with a tone that is often dismissive, condescending, and disdainful. Historians open to polemics now give way to polemists closed to history. "Grow up and join in—or pipe down and let us do it," contends British-born journalist Andrew Sullivan in a "long, long overdue" message addressed to "Europe's appeasers" on the eve of the war in Iraq.[21] As to Richard Perle, a leading member of the new anti-EU brigade, Europe's "numbing pacifism" and lost "moral fiber" have been cause for its decline—"in politics, economics, social and political life, and moral reasoning"—that is moving the Old World farther away from the United States.[22]

"Are we not better off because we wound up with something other than containment?" adds Perle, as a back-handed boast about policies advocated by the United States in the 1980s, but bitterly questioned or opposed by the European allies and many of their current leaders.[23] Why stop such indictment of Europe and its misguided policies with the Cold War, though? The "glorious" record built by the United States over time now reveals a distinctive American habit to save Europe from itself in war (in 1917 and 1941), without a thought for the indifference shown previous to, or early into, each conflict (in 1914 and 1939). This is court history at its worst.[24] Not limited to the enlightened U.S. policies adopted by President Truman after World War II, such praise is extended to the totality of the past century, from President Wilson who tried to move France away from its vengeful ways in 1919, to President Bush *père* who overcame a dangerous Anglo-French opposition to Germany's unification in 1989, and President Clinton who protected Europe from its own insufficiencies in Bosnia in the summer of 1995.

A main American casualty of the Cold War would be the idea of history, warned historian William A. Williams early on.[25] For Williams, this "idea" was nothing less than a measure of each nation's honesty and integrity in measuring its performance, not only relative to other Great Powers but also, and especially, relative to its own ideals and national sense of itself. Forty years later, the neoconservative indictment of Europe's history resurrects this warning at the expense of an Old World that is itself recalled with selective and even flawed memories of the past. Many Europeans can agree that they fought World War I with "a fervor . . . bordering on a religious experience."[26] To this day, that fervor remains a challenge to reason, as do the five suicidal years that followed. But even more Europeans would also take exception to the idea that World War II could have been prevented[27] had they been more willing to fight the evil regime in Germany, and could have been shortened had they not surrendered "with scarcely a fight"—after losses, notes historian Niall Ferguson, that "amounted to less than 1 percent of the prewar population."[28] In the heat of the post-9/11 policy debates, history is once again a main American casualty. In five weeks of fighting in the spring of 1940, the French suffered about 92,000 killed and about 200,000 wounded before acknowledging defeat and leaving it up to a few of them, regrouped in London, to salvage a small measure of national pride.[29] Granted that these losses are below Ferguson's odd criterion of "1 percent," the French fought, however ineffectively, while others regretfully slept—and even, to put it more crudely, they paid for their mistakes with their lives and dignity while others, who had insisted on loan repayments from past allies and sustained cozy relationships with future adversaries, cashed in for their indifference.[30]

Because Americans and Europeans cut across the past at different moments, their narratives do not quite intersect. An account of World War II that begins in December 1941 cannot apply the same standards of judgment as a European account that begins before—usually long before—August 1939, and ends after—usually long after—June 1944. In effect, the history of the interwar years produces enough shame to pass around broadly. France's defeat in 1940 was not due only to a lack of equipment or an unwillingness to fight, but also to inept military planning, discredited political leadership and, a mere twenty years after another world war, an understandable public wariness and widespread antiwar sentiments. These explain the "phony war" that delayed serious fighting for nearly nine months after war had been declared. But the French failings hardly tell the entire story of interwar follies, and the Nazi sweep of Europe cannot be attributed exclusively to the French surrender in June 1940—any more than to Belgium's earlier surrender or Finland's subsequent defeat.

These horrendous months of 1940, and the horrific war that followed, were also, and even primarily, the product of a broader failure of the West to build a cohesive alliance because of the self-serving assumption made by Britain (and the United States) that a French (or Anglo-French) military shield was enough to prevent, contain, or even defeat Germany. When that assumption proved to be wrong in August 1939, and even more so after June 1940, Britain fought with a spirit and a resilience that invite lasting admiration: as the year 1941 was coming to a painful end, partly healed by the promises of America's entry in the war, Britain and its Empire had already suffered over 180,000 casualties, including nearly 50,000 dead—not to mention the suffering endured stoically when Adolf Hitler began a systematic destruction of Britain's cities.[31]

That the first two years of the war against Hitler and his demonic ideas would have been fought while waiting for the United States to settle a bitter internal debate over its own participation is no cause for pride. Troubling, too, is the fact that the Roosevelt administration maintained full diplomatic relations with the Nazi regime that was praised by then-Ambassador to London, Joseph Kennedy, the father of a future president. After that, the war went on for another twenty-nine months, and caused millions more casualties, before U.S. forces landed in Normandy to write some of the most glorious pages of our nation's history. Yet, as the interwar history of Europe is now remembered amidst the new security challenges raised after the Cold War and since September 11, 2001, who showed the more deeply rooted habit of indifference and appeasement during the first half of the past century? Indeed, when the evil could no longer be ignored after Japan's surprise attack on Pearl Harbor, it is sad to remember that it was Hitler who declared war on the United States rather than the other way around.

On the eve of the transatlantic crisis of 2003 over Iraq, America's denunciation of Europe gained unprecedented intensity when it evoked "a millennium-old urge that powerfully infected and shaped European history" to present and explain "old" Europe's courting of Islam at the expense of the Jews.[32] "The richness of European culture," wrote George Will in the spring of 2002, is such that "even [Europe's] decadence is creative. Since 1945 it has produced the truly remarkable phenomenon of anti-Semitism without the Jews."[33] As if the charge was not sufficiently offensive, the formula was expanded into a broader attack against Europe's secularism in whose name "Christian anti-Semitism" can be unleashed "without the Christianity."[34] In the new melting pot of European prejudices thus restored to fit the current anti-European mood, the old—anti-religious and anti-Semite—and the new—anti-American—are combined to leave most of Europe unworthy of being America's friend. Thus liberated from Europe, America will finally be able to turn to "China, India, Mexico, Indonesia, Brazil, Vietnam, the Arab world, and Turkey" as the most appropriate partners "to huddle with most earnestly at important international conclaves—not Europe."[35]

"Preserve the myth" of NATO (or EU) relevance "and laugh,"[36] high U.S. officials were reportedly saying on the eve of military action in Iraq, after a war in Afghanistan which the United States also chose to wage mainly alone even after the NATO allies had unanimously offered to help.[37] In the past, such U.S. declarations would have pointed to a new isolationism—*laissez-les faire*, but without us; now, they reflect a new interventionism *à l'américaine*, that is, *sans* the Europeans. "If the old alliance is gone," wrote Jeff Gedmin, "it's time to start building something new"—with non-EU members like "the Eastern Europeans, the Turks and Israelis," and (as a telling afterthought) "the Brits . . . [who] can help enormously if they guard their independence from Brussels."[38] In the end, therefore, anti-Americanism in Europe has finally found its match in the United States where a strong Euro-phobic strand, which began to emerge amidst fears that the Cold War might be lost, and gathered momentum after the U.S. triumph over the Soviet Union, has gained new and widespread legitimacy since September 2001.

While America may still like Europe but does not seem to like Europeans much, Europe likes Americans but does not seem to like America much—or what it is said to stand for. That at least may look like an improvement over earlier days, when the "ugly American" reigned—"unloved" because "voracious, preachy, mercenary, and bombastically chauvinistic."[39] The tone was disturbing. "Americans," wrote Vincent Auriol, the first president of the French Fourth Republic, are "naïve, ignorant, and understand nothing."[40] Thirty years later, another French socialist leader about to be elected president, François Mitterrand, found such traits appealing (*"sympathiques"*). His concerns, however, were frankly more political than intellectual. "I like Americans," Mitterrand claimed, "but not their policies. . . . I note," he added, possibly carried away by the partisan rhetoric needed for his domestic alliance with the Communist Party, "that the United States has not ceased waging an economic war against us."[41] Later, Mitterrand was a spokesman for much of Europe when he dismissed President Reagan as "a man without ideas and without culture" but, small blessing, with "great good sense and profoundly good intentions."[42]

Similar pronouncements were made elsewhere in Europe and throughout the Cold War. Predictably, they were best heard in the United States when they carried a French accent. But that was not just a French view. After World War II, there had been Britain. "Does Britain like us?" anxiously asked one of *Newsweek*'s postwar "special reports" in late 1947.[43] In the United States, the question was understandably astonishing: the Truman administration had just made an unprecedented commitment to the reconstruction of Britain and its European neighbors. Yet with one out of three Englishmen said to be anti-American, the illness had reportedly "spread from the wealthy and intellectual classes down into the lower middle and working-class strata." Denis W. Brogan, Britain's early guru of anti-Americanism, was already warning against an emerging "omnipotence of American power." As Brogan put it, "Forced to live . . . in a world they definitely thought they had killed in its cradle . . . the average American is uneasy, ready to believe that the cause of all his discontents is treason or folly of his rulers, unwilling to accept the fact that the world was not made exclusively by or for Americans."[44]

Why go on? Whether attributable to a few countries and their culture, or their institutions and their people, Europe's ambivalence about the United States has been a persistent feature of transatlantic relations. Being an American in most parts of Europe is not unlike being a Frenchman in most parts of America, or an Italian in most parts of Germany, or a German in most parts of Britain: not a death sentence, to be sure, but certainly a life sentence. Upon his arrival in the United States in the 1950s, professor Stanley Hoffmann found it "easier to be French abroad than in France," because it is in the United States that he could best uncover his "Frenchness."[45] The same was true of U.S. citizens who traveled to Europe after the war, and always found the experience challenging. "It was the American in myself I stumbled upon while trying to discover Europe," thought Norman Podhoretz in the 1950s. "For protest as we all might . . . we were in a million small details marked off . . . as an identifiable national type."[46] Indeed, it was true. Europe's disdainful view of America's intellectual life always came together with a skeptical look at America's "right" to lead, as well as a sharply critical look at America's political right. In fact, what Europe may now resent most about America is that it responds too well to the historic image Europe has of itself. In other words, the resentment is not about what America has become but over what Europe itself has ceased to be—dominant, domineering, and sure of itself.

Europe's obsessive anti-American reflex—or tale or fable or ploy— may be generally boring and specifically offensive in the United States, but it has been over the years on the whole inconsequential. Even if America's current views of Europe reflect its rising exasperation over Europe's own resentment of America, many other concerns compound that resentment and place Europe's anti-Americanism and America's anti-Europeanism on parallel tracks. For some, anti-Americanism is just a matter of ideology as it is alleged that Europe directs its venom most directly to republican conservatives—their leaders and their "belief in individualism, liberty and self-reliance."[47] That view is reinforced by post–Cold War transatlantic tensions that are especially more pronounced on the new societal agenda of values-oriented issues than on foreign policy and security issues. For others, it is a matter of attitude, as the ghosts of Europe's past grandeur that are still sighted amidst the ruins of its decline supposedly motivate Europe's quest for renewed power and influence in an anti-American multipolar world. Alternatively, even as these aspirations are shown to be hollow, they are replaced by an arrogant pride in Europe's willingness to relinquish the sovereignty of its nation-states to institutions that make of their continent the new New World, as opposed to the aging New World across the Atlantic. Finally, for a few others, anti-Americanism is a pervasive plot, usually carried out by France (often with Germany but in spite of Britain) on behalf of a narrow view of Europe that wants to be asserted at the expense of a U.S.-led NATO.[48]

This exercise in mutual schizophrenia ("Go home, but don't leave us.") and paranoia ("Why don't you love us?") illustrates the ambivalence shown by each side of the Atlantic toward the other. That ambivalence is multidimensional. At the broadest level, it involves America's comfort zone with Europe—united but up to a point, and strong but also without excess. That, in the end, explains the U.S. interest in privileged partners that can isolate challengers to its leadership—as tentatively captured by de Gaulle's image of a Trojan horse brought into Europe via Britain to give the then-nascent European Community the American influence it was expected to balance or at least resist. However, even that is hardly a U.S. "plot" designed to ensure its hegemony. Rather, it reflects a U.S. concern over the consequences of Europe's failure—the sense, sharpened by past experiences, that where America is comprised of fully "united" states that pursue a single foreign and security policy, Europe remains a fragmented union of disunited states whose role in the world is limited by their inability to develop a common, let alone single, foreign and security policy. The United States must, therefore, keep the rein short lest the European allies be tempted, once again, to start something they could not end—whether a war or a revolution—but that America could not ignore because of the interests at stake—to win the war or contain the revolution.

But to unprecedented levels, Europe's comfort zone with America also reflects a deep and pervasive concern over the consequences of America's failures. In other words, now, in the post-9/11 world, as before during the Cold War, Europe is prepared to applaud any U.S. policy as soon as it has worked, but now more than ever before the states of Europe are reluctant to remain passive and powerless should the expected success fail to materialize. The stakes have grown. Thus, even as America bemoans Europe's weakness, Europe fears America's power. While young Americans deplore what Europe is and has ceased to be, young Europeans question what America has become and does. In 1999, the Kosovo conflict served as a vivid reminder of lingering Hobbesian instincts that a neo-Kantian institutional reality in Europe has not fully tamed. That conflict, it should be remembered, was initially expected to be short and relatively pain free—an exercise in cooperative bombing whereby America and its allies would do what they had said they would so that Serbia could be forced to do what it had said it would not do. Instead, it lasted eleven weeks, involved live coverage of NATO bombing of a European capital that had stood up to both Hitler and Stalin, and the total devastation of a coastline that had become one of Europe's most coveted summer destinations.

Europeans know well how devastating American military power can be when unleashed in war—especially those wars they started out of alleged necessity and which Americans joined in the name of justice. This is not to suggest that any of the global wars waged in and over Europe in the twentieth century were America's responsibility. The opposite is known to be true. Considered individually or collectively, these wars have left a moral debt that Europe will not be able to redeem for generations to come, and even then history will insist that no such debt can ever be paid in full. But the killing of civilians is not limited to the historically failed continental Great Powers in Europe or the new barbaric rogue states elsewhere in the world. The one-night bombing of Dresden, in March 1945, killed more German civilians than the Korean War and the Vietnam War combined killed American armed combatants—and by the time evil had been exorcized in Nazi Germany, about 600,000 German civilians had been killed amidst the ruins of an estimated 3.5 million destroyed homes.[49] If Europe fears the U.S. military and understates the relevance of military power, it is not out of anger at the country that has done most to save them from their own wars—"insensibility," it is written of the defeated Germans, "was the condition for their success"—but because it has spent too much of its recent history recovering from the damages caused by those who had to destroy them in order to save them.

But is Europe's anti-Americanism now taken too seriously in the United States? Certainly, a spreading "hatred" of Americans around the world is cause for legitimate concern. But that hatred does not apply to Europe, where anti-Americanism may be an exasperating attitude, an occasional ideological project, or an effective political tactic, but it is not a broad indictment of America. Unlike other anti-Americans who question what is best, not worst, in America—democracy, tolerance, the rights of women, and much more—anti-Americans in Europe cherish what is best in the United States, and mainly challenge societal flaws that are deplored by large numbers of Americans as well—the lack of gun control, for example, or an insufficient protection of the environment, or the lack of medical coverage for all, to cite but a few of the issues that define partisan differences in the United States.[50] If that is an appropriate definition of anti-Americanism, then about half of all Americans are anti-American as well.

Before September 11, 2001, anti-Americanism in Europe addressed a host of U.S. initiatives that were designed to end the Cold War but which many in Europe feared for their provocative potential, especially with regard to defeated states like Russia, ascending powers like China, or rogue states like North Korea. Since September 11, priorities have changed but, surprisingly, transatlantic differences over existing threats and priorities have not increased and they may even have receded.[51] What has changed instead is that Europeans have grown on the whole more cautious as they deny the urgency of the threat (except in the case of the Israeli-Palestinian conflict), while on the whole Americans have become more prone to take risks as they emphasize the imminence of the new threats and the legitimacy of preemption as a vital tool of action, especially with regard to the proliferation of weapons of mass destruction and at the expense of terrorist regimes or groups that receive the support of such regimes. But even when the threat is viewed with the same urgency, differences remain over the most effective ways to address and reduce it—whether with military force or with diplomatic, humanitarian, and peacekeeping missions. In other words, what is challenged are not the facts of American preponderant power but its competence in light of America's ways of history, its phobias, and its supposedly inexperienced leaders.

I hear you, like you, and lead you—and neither do I. So goes America's dialogue with Europe, and Europe's dialogue with America. More than ever, this dialogue consists of two monologues that are misheard and misrepresented. Should this condition continue, the transatlantic rift that erupted in 2002 and grew into an unprecedented crisis in 2003 could drift, past Iraq and beyond Bush, into an irreversible transatlantic divide that would unleash the very sort of American unilateralism that Europe fears. To avoid such an unwanted outcome, America will have to be judged for what it does and has done, and Europe will have to be seen for what it is and has become—the former to explain more effectively that the leadership it asserts is not intended to dominate and remains open to needed adjustments, and the latter to demonstrate that the followership it offers is not intended to obstruct and is ready for cooperation. In short, exasperated Americans should understand at last that U.S. interests in Europe are too significant to be left to apprehensive Europeans alone, but apprehensive Europeans should also understand that a continued U.S. interest in Europe is too important to be left to exasperated Americans alone.

To this extent, Europe's anti-Americanism, which feeds this condition, may well be "an obsession," but it is an obsession that is no longer benign.[52] The West won the Cold War because America was able to convert the world, including Europe, to its own faith in anticommunism and the values threatened by the Soviet Union. The risk for the West now would be to lose the war against terrorism by making it possible for Europe (and the world) to embrace an ill-defined but tempting phobia known as anti-Americanism while the United States responds to its own temptation to go it alone or without its allies of choice.

NEITHER TERROR NOR WAR

The transatlantic gap revealed by these two monologues—delivered separately but heard simultaneously—was significantly widened by the existential security risks unveiled by the events of September 11, 2001. Neither acts of war proper, nor mere terrorist actions, these events point to a novel definition of what constitutes a threat to national or international security—a new approach to the use of force and, by implication, a new kind of warfare, new challenges to the capacity for retribution—where and when—and, by implication, a new sort of deterrence. As a result of 9/11, Americans lost the sense of territorial security and individual safety that had distinguished the United States from other countries in the past. (Except during the Cuban missile crisis in late 1962, the risk of a Soviet nuclear attack against the United States was never seriously feared, or feared for long. In the case of the missile crisis, the U.S. reaction was to preempt the threat raised by the deployment of a large number of the Soviet strategic forces closer to its intended targets in U.S. territory, and while no regime change was truly attempted, Fidel Castro is still paying for his impudence forty years after the fact.)

The impact of September 11 on transatlantic relations was worsened by Europe's inability to appreciate its enduring consequences on the United States and its people. Whether the world was directly changed by these events can be debated, to be sure, but however this debate is settled it should have been clear that America's view of the world would be deeply transformed by what transpired on that day. In a sense, this is the first time in at least seventy years that America is fighting a war in its own name and on its own behalf—to protect the nation's territory, to restore the security of its citizens, and to cater to its own interests in the face of an aggression that must be answered. None of this could be said of most wars waged by the United States in the twentieth century. Even Japan's attack at Pearl Harbor was not deemed repeatable throughout the forty-four-month war that followed, whereas fears of another attack now haunt America and its citizens, not only in U.S. territory but wherever else they might be. Living in the fear of war and terror may be common, and thus even tolerable, in most parts of the world, but it is new, and not readily acceptable, in the United States.

Coming soon after the harsh criticism of George W. Bush earlier in the year, Europe's spontaneous response to these events was extraordinary. It involved not only the unprecedented invocation of Article V of the North Atlantic Treaty, but also an equally impressive demonstration of "total solidarity" from the fifteen members of the European Union, as well as the use of European influence to ensure swift UN support for the United States. Shared values and overlapping interests among like-minded allies were creating a community of action that had been lacking previously, when the allies were waiting for war to come to them from the East, rather than making preparations to bring war to the enemy wherever it might be. Yet the U.S. surprise in the face of this institutional triple play was itself surprising: If not from Europe, from where? Even critics who question the reality of the Euro-Atlantic geographic space as a community of values and interests acknowledge it as a community of virtues—that is, a group of states that share a body of self-evident truths that are known by all, and known to be common to all even when they are not endorsed evenly by all.[53]

The transatlantic schism that developed soon after in 2002, and reached such unprecedented intensity in 2003 as to seem potentially fatal in 2004, calls for some explanation. There was more to this crisis than Europe's mistrust of the U.S. president, however deep it was upon his inauguration in January 2001. For one, the dust in New York had barely settled when the allies in Europe became increasingly ambivalent about the scope and goals of the U.S. reaction in and beyond Afghanistan. With the history of the Old World serving as reference for the events that had transpired in the New World, many in Europe minimized their significance by insisting on the tragic normalcy of interstate relations, as they had known it during their own history. After all, war is a way of life for Great Powers, and terror is a recurring accident that can be defeated when it erupts and must be forgotten after it has been controlled. For another, Europeans could claim that fighting terrorism was nothing new within their borders. To be or not to be at war—the semantic contest that began almost at once between the United States and the states of Europe pointed to a strategic gap that was all the more likely to expand as no serious effort was made to bridge it, especially as America was preparing for a war in Iraq that, surprisingly, many in Europe still expected to avoid or prevent in early 2003.[54]

Yet, whatever word might be used to describe the attacks of September 11, and however well these attacks might be said to fit the ways of history, it is not the American way. Accordingly, President George W. Bush insisted that the "new normalcy" that had been threatened on September 11 would have to be defeated without conditions, and even preempted without compassion.[55] On January 29, 2002, the yearly State of the Union message, designed to address domestic constituencies, aroused Europe's concerns and led transatlantic relations to take a turn for the worse. What caused offense in that speech was its form as well as its substance—not only what Bush said (and how he said it), but also what he might do (and how he would do it). Coming barely three months after the impressive display of solidarity through NATO, the EU, and the United Nations, the president's failure to give these institutions their due, compared to his effusive praise for the likes of Pakistan's president Pervez Musharaff, was astonishing—the first in a series of political mistakes that could have been avoided, but were not. Mistaken, too, was the provocative linkage between Iran, Iraq, and North Korea—an "axis of evil," claimed Bush, which left most of continental Europe fearful of where the United States intended to act next, whether because other terrorist attacks might aim at soft European targets, or because of U.S. reprisals that might aim at targets dangerously close to Europe. To complicate matters further, the president's reference to a "terrorist underworld . . . including groups like Hamas, Hezballah, Islamic Jihad, and Jaish-I-Muhammad" read mostly like Israeli Prime Minister Ariel Sharon's hit list—an ominous sign at a time when Europe was growing restless over the U.S. neglect of the Middle East. Altogether, the State of the Union speech deepened the allies' apprehension that, as had been shown in Afghanistan, they were moved to a secondary role even for issues with which they were directly concerned and which they were committed to defeat in coordination with, but not under the subjugation of, their senior partner across the Atlantic.

For Europe, there was also a not-so-small matter of Bush-bashing. Thus, Europe's characterization of the new U.S. president as inexperienced, ill prepared, and mostly incompetent often crossed the boundaries of tolerable language. At best, President Bush was said to be a younger version of Ronald Reagan—a comparison that was not meant to be flattering—and his "axis of evil" speech was promptly linked to Reagan's battle with the "evil empire" a generation earlier, boosted by allegations that the president was showing a puerile desire to attend to security matters left unfinished by his father during the first war in the Gulf ten years earlier.[56] Yet, more than Ronald Reagan or Bush's father, the younger Bush was echoing Harry S. Truman, who had not been Europe's favorite in his early days either. In March 1947, it was also in a Message to Congress that Truman had evoked the new security normalcy shaped by the rise of the Soviet threat to America's security as well as to its way of life. A passive satisfaction with the containment of additional Soviet expansion was not, and never became, the exclusive dimension of Truman's policies, however. Throughout, regime change was an implicit U.S. goal that raised more risks when Moscow began to acquire its own weapons of mass destruction, together with the capabilities needed to deliver them, first on targets throughout Europe and next on targets in the United States. Containing the Soviet Union would ultimately, and even inevitably, bring about a rollback of its regime. To this end, a North Atlantic alliance was organized, to which was added, eighteen months later, an organization that would give it the military tools needed to satisfy the goals to which the original twelve alliance members had subscribed. A few years later, six European members of the Alliance signed the Rome Treaties, thus reinforcing the multilateral strands of a multidimensional alliance within which economic reconstruction, political rehabilitation, and military security were sought distinctively but could not be achieved separately. It took ten years and one military buildup to develop that alliance in a genuinely integrated military organization, and another thirty-five-odd years (and at least two more military buildups) to ensure its triumph with the peaceful reunification of Germany, the collapse of the Soviet Empire, and the birth of a European Union in 1992.

To combat the new, post-9/11 security conditions, Bush sought to rely on the overwhelming abundance of American military power for the many missions that were needed for victory to be achieved. Bush's messianic view of the world—"with us or against us" in a battle explicitly designed to exorcize a new "evil" and "bring him to justice . . . dead or alive"—paralleled Truman's vision of the world, as he had presented it in March 1947.[57] Like Truman's, Bush's strategy was global—"wherever they are"—and time consuming as it called on Americans to remain, in George Kennan's words, "steadfast and patient and persistent." Finally, and also like Truman, Bush, with a knowledge of history limited to that which he has lived, drew from these fragmented memories of the past the strength of his convictions and the passion of his emotions. Truman was a product of World War I (in which he courageously fought) and Munich (which he bitterly deplored), and President Bush was, in his words, "a product of the Vietnam era" (even though this was a war in which he did not serve and from which he did not dissent—a war, in other words, to which he had remained on the whole indifferent). As he later confided in order to explain his post-9/11 mindset: "I remember presidents trying to wage wars that were very unpopular, and the nation split. . . . I had the job of making sure the American people understood . . . the severity of the attack."[58] In short, Bush concluded in February 2002, "this nation won't rest until we have destroyed terrorism. . . . I can't tell you how passionate I feel on the subject. . . . There is no calendar, there is no deadline."[59] That conclusion still prevailed as the "war after the war" in Iraq took unexpected turns in 2004 and, about to celebrate the sixtieth anniversary of the Normandy landings, President Bush came to build surprising parallels between the war in Iraq and World War II—parallels that many in Europe found not only "simplistic" but also frankly offensive.

There, however, ends the comparison. Having scared the hell out of the American people (as Truman had been urged to do) to "make sure they understood" the severity of the postwar challenge they faced, Truman quickly looked the other way as he ignored his own doctrine wherever it seemed at issue—from the coup in Czechoslovakia to the communist revolution in China—and learned to keep wars limited wherever he thought he had to wage them, including Korea. Moreover, Truman's multilateral framework grouped complementary institutions that included a military organization built on U.S. power and a European project based on Franco-German reconciliation—as well as a United Nations organization that was expected to respond to U.S. leadership. In truth, Truman was an architect. Whatever was still unfinished in the blueprint he left in January 1953 was quickly enacted by Dwight D. Eisenhower and occasionally refurbished and enlarged by his successors. By comparison, President Bush seemed to lack a vision of the alliance, as he grudgingly accepted it as a viable option only after he had considered available alternatives with a new cluster of coalition partners rendered available and willing by the end of the Cold War.

Throughout, Truman was also a determined keeper of a presidency he knew he had assumed fortuitously and temporarily. After April 1945, his sensitivity to the circumstances that had brought him to the presidency made him especially cautious until he was elected on his own in November 1948. Yet Truman understood full well the need for leadership during these early postwar years, when the main constraints faced by the nation came from within rather than from the world without. In other words, granted that America was vulnerable to the new threat raised by Soviet prewar ideology and postwar power, that vulnerability was no less moral and political than physical and territorial. But that threat was hardly self-evident. This was indeed a war, but it was a "cold" war: the enemy was elusive, the interests ill defined, and the risks murky—a war that could be viewed as a war of choice, which the American people were made to perceive as a necessary war on the basis of a presidential rhetoric that admittedly overstated both the reality and the urgency of the Soviet threat.

Bush, too, initially gained the presidency under unusual conditions—as a minority president who had received half a million votes fewer than his opponent. But unlike Truman, Bush never doubted his legitimacy and lost no time in embracing the full authority of his office.[60] And in any case, unlike Truman, the need for war could not be denied after September 11, 2001. Where Truman had meant to protect America's security for the long term, Bush now needed to restore it and save the nation in the short term—"save civilization itself," he claimed like Truman—from the consequences of indifference of failure. Given the enormity of the "vitriolic hatred of America" that inspired the terrorist threat, there was to be no mercy.[61] The security risk had been elevated, and so was, therefore, the president's willingness to take risks on behalf of the nation as he pleaded to "round up" or "smoke out" an enemy that would be brought to justice "dead or alive" and wherever he was or might be found. In 2002, Bush's vision and related warnings proved to be enough to rally the American people around their president, à la Truman, but over time they might also scare everybody else. This latter risk of alienation, which was apparent as preparations for war in Iraq started, grew when it appeared that prewar planning had bordered on self-deception and theology, and when it was revealed that postwar practices had little to do with known traditions of compassion and fairness, even when these traditions were presented as covers for various conservative or liberal strands of realpolitik.[62]

Thus, while 9/11 changed America's vision of the world, making it more dangerous and hostile, the war in Iraq changed the world's vision of America, making America itself more dangerous and hostile. That condition is likely to endure because the conditions that caused it are not likely to end soon. Yet the reality is that notwithstanding the world's new concerns about America, there is still a pro-American world out there, a world that respects its need for an America it can enjoy and admire even when, on occasion, it cannot avoid fearing and resenting it. For unlike most other countries that enjoyed such power in the past, being liked is what Americans do well and like best: their goal is truly to reach and gain the souls and minds of the defeated people, rather than to exploit their lands and seize their assets. "After defeating enemies," observed President Bush on the eve of the war against Iraq, "we do not leave behind occupying armies, we leave constitutions and parliaments."[63] Europe is a case in point, and yet it is Europe's understanding that America may be lacking most at this critical juncture.

3

IN DEFENSE OF
AMERICAN POLICIES

It is with reminiscences of President Truman's commitment to a bold and extravagant vision of a new Europe that rests a preliminary defense of American policies. For it is to the extent that the European idea of an ever closer Europe also became an American idea that six European heads of state and government were able to launch the long and tedious process that stands as one of the most successful U.S. foreign policies ever.

Nearly half a century later, there should be considerable satisfaction on both sides of the Atlantic. In Rome, in March 1957, the countries united in this effort understood their purpose—to end war—better than they anticipated the full potential of their commitment—to end the nation-state. The fears that dominated that moment were shaped by the innumerable wars these nations had fought on each other, often at the expense, or because, of their neighbors, as well as their own. Admittedly, the idea of European unity was not new. In 1929, a romantic and quickly forgotten speech delivered at the League of Nations had proposed the creation of a United States of Europe. It had been written by a French poet, St. John Perse, who worked for another poet, Foreign Minister Aristide Briand. But for the decades that followed, little of that poetry could be heard in the camps and gulags that hosted an entire generation of Europeans who happened to live on the wrong side of the Rhine, of the Oder River, or of the Pyrénées, and who embraced the wrong faith, the wrong ideology, or the wrong country.

In 1957, however, amidst the ruins left by a war that had ended only twelve years earlier, there could be no hope for renewal without a touch of poetic idealism. For the nations of postwar Europe to remain "prisoners of their recent quarrels, inconsolable because of their vanished greatness, brooding bitterly over their losses, boasting of their culture and their past, finding morose in their decadence" was a certain recipe for more disasters.[1] A new approach was needed to end the thirty-year war that had begun in August 1914 and had brought death to the Old World. Absent that approach, Europe was doomed to everlasting silence, so complete was its collapse and so hopeless its future.

Admittedly, only Europeans could give this approach the political reality it needed. These were leaders of conviction—"European saints" whose names linger side by side with those of their counterparts in the Truman administration.[2] There was Jean Monnet, whose perseverance and uncanny ability to make converts "one by one," in government and in the private sector proved decisive.[3] For legitimacy, Monnet had an unsurpassed network of friends in the United States, where Dean Acheson embraced him as "one of the greatest of Frenchmen,"[4] not the least, perhaps, for the elegant knowledge of English he had gained during his prewar years in America, but also, and most of all, for his imaginative and far-reaching proposals on behalf of European unity.[5] For domestic political support, Monnet could count on Robert Schuman, a pillar of the French Fourth Republic, who soon became "the living embodiment of Franco-German amity."[6] Schuman, who spoke French with a German accent but German with no accent, found an indispensable German interlocutor in Konrad Adenauer, a "cunning idealist" who gambled that locking his country's future into Europe was the most effective way to master Germany's past.[7] Then as now, the magic of history knew no limits: the father of Germany's new democracy was elected in the newly formed Bundestag by one vote only, which he cast himself. To tame Germany's instincts on the vital issue of unification, Adenauer engineered a strategy of silence that, he knew, could give him security from adversaries and legitimacy with friends abroad, while keeping him in power at home. Like Schuman and Adenauer, Alcide de Gasperi, the Italian, had also grown or lived in disputed border areas where he, too, gained the outlook needed to mount a collective assault on the nationalist forces that would otherwise stand in the way of a lasting recovery—de Gasperi, who had sat in the Imperial Reichtag in Vienna where he represented the Alto Adige region; Schuman in Luxembourg and then Lorraine, when both lay in the German Empire; and even Adenauer, who had thought about Rhineland separatism in post-1919 Germany. There were many others—like, especially, Paul-Henry Spaak, the Belgian, who often conversed with Adenauer and Schuman in German, and hoped to transcend his small country's limits within an integrated European system where each nation's size would not determine its influence.

This was an extraordinary generation of bold European leaders, but none of their hopes and little of their endeavor could succeed without significant U.S. support. The United States was the indispensable partner, not only in the absence of any viable alternative but also because of an implicit understanding that the power that could be found across the Atlantic served those very values that Europeans had themselves betrayed during the previous years. For Americans about to engage in the little-known tasks of postwar reconstruction, the nation-states of Europe were cumbersome and dangerous. By comparison, the idea of Europe looked like a convincing attempt to reconfigure the Old World to the image of the new—as had been done when the thirteen American colonies expanded into an ever closer and ever larger union of their own. However old the idea might be, now, in 1945, it was an idea whose time had come at last.[8] The legacies of two world wars had left a triumphant America and a fading Europe with three daunting tasks: the rehabilitation of defeated enemies, the reconstruction of destroyed economies among victorious and vanquished states alike, and the reconciliation of historic enemies. Indeed, Truman and his administration intuitively understood—perhaps better than most of their European interlocutors—that all three tasks were explicitly dependent on a radical transformation of Europe without which there could be none of the order to which American power was now fully committed.

MULTILATERALISM WITHOUT TEARS

After World War II, America's rise as a world power was neither an ambition nor a vocation. Rather, there was a broadly understood need to tame the anarchy that had forced America to enter two wars in and beyond Europe during the previous thirty-odd years.

The hegemonic consequences of the U.S. response to this condition were neither intended nor welcomed. The Truman Doctrine, announced in the spring of 1947, had a global reach, but the president's subsequent decisions paralleled the ambivalence of the American public and the limits of American power. These decisions responded to explicit European requests and needs: they aimed at making their beneficiaries in the West so prosperous and stable as to end war among them while inducing their communist neighbors in the East to emulate rather than attack them. It is only after the 1948 presidential elections in America, with the signing of the Washington Treaty in April 1949, the birth of the Federal Republic of Germany in October 1949, and the outbreak of the Korean War in June 1950, that Truman began to bridge the gap between his discourse and his actions. In September 1950, the Atlantic Alliance was given an organization (NATO) that ultimately helped its members to fulfill all of their stated goals—to keep an expansionist Russia out, a divided Germany subdued, and a distant America engaged. In future years, alliances were also concluded elsewhere, in Asia and in the Middle East, where other countries linked their interests to the forward deployment of U.S. forces as substitutes for the defeated imperial powers of Europe. But none of these alliances matched the scope of the commitments and the depth of the commonalities that made the Atlantic Alliance vital, and even special, from the start.

Whatever their inspiration, these policies served America and its allies well. Neither the U.S. indifference to the world during the post-1919 years, nor the world's indifference to the United States during the pre-1914 years was a credible option. Europe's resistance to some U.S. goals, especially with regard to Germany (which the United States wanted to rearm) and residual imperial holdings in Africa and Asia (which the United States wanted to liberate), and confusion about some of the American thinking, especially over the dilution of national sovereignty within U.S.-sponsored multilateral institutions, were overcome.[9] The imperatives of economic, military, and political support for reconstruction in, protection of, and reconciliation within Europe were compelling, and only the United States had the capabilities and the will to provide that support. In early 1947, the main danger for Europe was not Germany, in whatever territorial shape, but a united Germany under Soviet influence: by extension, the only hope for Europe was a security system that would be built with the United States, without the Soviet Union, and even in spite of the European nation-states.[10]

In the United States, Truman's decisions motivated the nation's first "great debate" about the U.S. role in the postwar world, a confused debate that internationalists easily won over their isolationist interlocutors. The fact that the debate was waged in the name of a realism that endorsed the need for power so long as it was used on behalf of ideals compatible with American vital interests and national purpose added to the confusion: neither power without justice, nor justice without power, but interests guided by justice and enforced by power. Over the years, U.S. leaders often made their policies sound easier (meaning cost free) and more altruistic (meaning oblivious to national interests) than they were. As a result, the general public could not readily understand the interventionist pain that was endured along the way, especially after the war in Korea had escalated from a small "police action" against North Korea into a major conventional war with China and a global Cold War with the Soviet Union. Yet whatever setbacks U.S. policies faced, they built a multilateral order that was endorsed readily as no ally could raise meaningful obstacles to the exercise of U.S. leadership within the institutions to which they now belonged. This was, therefore, multilateralism without tears—less a commitment to consult than a willingness to inform, at a time and over issues mainly of America's own choosing.

Whatever hegemonic innocence may be claimed on behalf of Truman and his intentions at the start of the Cold War, no benign characterization can be made of the Nixon years a generation later. By January 1969, the U.S. status as a dominant world power was beyond doubt, and isolationism had long ceased to be a realistic option. Accordingly, the new "great debate" that emerged during the Vietnam War involved almost exclusively internationalists who all shared a commitment to sustaining America's role in the world but disagreed profoundly over the ways in which that role ought to be played.[11] Ideas of empire slowly emerged, but without ideological preconceptions and in the power-based context of a "Pax

Americana" tied not only to the preponderance of U.S. capabilities but also to the scope of its interests and the reach of its values. To many, however, the idea had a bad scent and went against the drift of the nation's history. As written at the time, "One must [not] be an isolationist to protest against an imperial destiny for America, particularly an imperial destiny that results in the kind of war we have waged in Vietnam." But others, like Henry Kissinger, still struggled with that "destiny" as they explained the failure in Vietnam not as one of intent but as one of efficacy rooted in an "American philosophy of international relations" that needed to be revised "if we are not going to have another disaster that may have a quite different look but will have the same essential flaws."[12]

That American power and purpose were being tested in a country, Vietnam, and even a region, Southeast Asia, which had been kept outside the permissive consensus built since 1945, added to the intensity of the debate. As a setting for military intervention, a divided Korea had been understood as a proxy for a divided Germany, and by extension Europe, and Korea therefore stood as Europe's (and hence, America's) first line of defense. The inability to make the same argument in the case of South Vietnam made it increasingly difficult to defend the escalation of the war. Yet then, and even more so later, the critics' mistake was to misrepresent a specific case against the war in Vietnam as a general case against war anywhere.[13] That the Vietnam War had been a bad limited war did not imply that all limited wars should be avoided. That American power had been used ineffectively there did not imply that American power could no longer be effective elsewhere. As was noted at the time, "If the United States comes out of the military confrontation in Asia . . . with a sharpened sense of how to differentiate its role and distribute the various components of national power in the different areas of the world, it will have ascended to the crucial and perhaps last step toward the plateau of maturity. It will then have . . . become a true empire."[14]

On the path to imperial maturity, the Nixon-Kissinger foreign policy administration sought a new formula for global order—less centered on the availability of American power (and the will to use it) and more reliant on allies (and their restored capacity to build their own capabilities). To be sure, this was not a matter of choice. By temperament, Kissinger and the president he served trusted the nation's own power more than they did that of their allies. But denied the military capabilities and the political will needed to fulfill commitments that had expanded steadily since 1945, the Nixon administration was neither disposed to doing less (meaning no disengagement except from Vietnam) nor opposed to doing things differently (including détente with the Soviet Union and normalization with China). Instead, preponderance would be maintained on the cheap, thanks to the orchestrated contributions of reconstructed European allies, united and thus stronger but still grateful and thus faithful, and thanks, too, to regional viceroys that could be found among the newly influential countries of the post-Vietnam world. As Kissinger put it in April 1975, "A more fluid and complex world, with many centers of power, more subtle dangers, and more hopeful opportunities" called for a more fluid and more complex strategy that acknowledged the depletion of the postwar surplus of American power and will at a time when other countries in the world—allies and adversaries alike—could now do more.

To the extent that vocal public support at home was needed for such a strategy to work abroad, Kissinger's rhetoric was too geopolitical too early—in the realpolitik sense of the term, but also in the American sense of the time.[15] Yet, the U.S. geopolitical vision of the world had not fundamentally changed since the formative postwar years. If anything, the rise of Soviet military power and the spread of communist ideology confirmed Truman's earlier warnings, and made the world even more dangerous (though possibly less hostile) than before. But the United States had changed, and these changes seemed to matter even more than changes in the world. For the tragic escalation of the war in Vietnam had caused an agonizing reappraisal of America's self-image from within as well as throughout the world—a reappraisal that muted the omnipotent sounds of the Truman Doctrine and deflated the domineering call to arms eloquently issued by President Kennedy upon his inauguration in January 1961.

Kissinger was the first American scholar in a commanding position since Woodrow Wilson, but unlike Wilson, his scholarship in the art of manipulative diplomacy was traditional—that is, rooted in Europe, like Kissinger himself.[16] Echoing the 1815 Congress of Vienna, which had settled the Napoleonic wars, Kissinger sounded a bit like Talleyrand, the French foreign minister who had gone to Vienna in 1815 as if he had personally won a war lost by the nation he represented, and a bit like

Metternich, the Austrian chancellor whose dominant presence in Vienna had been inspired by what he knew to be the crumbling nature of an empire at the mercy of the next war. Hampered by a war that America had lost, thereby disrupting the nation and its institutions, Kissinger was no Bismarck, who had come to Paris in 1871 to impose peace terms after a war he had won (unlike Talleyrand) and which he knew he could easily win again (unlike Metternich). Yet the post-Vietnam world had little to do with post-1815 Europe, when the men gathered in Vienna had all been, in Kissinger's words, "products of essentially the same culture, professing the same ideals, sharing similar tastes."[17] Not only were these men alike, the countries they served were also alike: they all understood each other—the language they spoke, the interests they sought, the actions they took. But now, such homogeneity could be found neither at home, where memories of Vietnam haunted a sharply divided nation, nor abroad, where the sad spectacle of an America astray made adversaries in the East more assertive and occasionally bellicose, allies less responsive and occasionally adversarial, and new influences in the South more indifferent and occasionally hostile.

The new Kissingerian design for U.S. primacy and world order was, therefore, broadly ignored abroad and soon forgotten at home. America's adversaries viewed détente as a hard-earned opportunity to enhance their claims for parity—meaning more global influence—now that they had gained the military power they had lacked after World War II. Handpicked viceroys in the Third World dismissed the self-serving notion that they would do America's bidding in the regions under their control—like Iran in the Persian Gulf and, eventually, Iraq too. Across the Atlantic, Kissinger's "Year of Europe," announced in 1973, wanted the European allies to reinforce their role in the world: the call was not heard, and when heard it was generally misrepresented as a U.S. attempt to take over an ascending Europe. More pointedly, another war in the Middle East later in the year, and the first oil crisis for several years afterward, made Kissinger's first attempt at a broad transformation of the Alliance moot anyway.

The Year of Europe was accordingly tabled, but the U.S. tentative search for a new multilateralism extended with the European allies, and applied beyond Europe, was not abandoned. Rather, it was revised—first by the Carter administration because of Kissinger's alleged mishandling of the ascending powers in the Third World (and his neglect of the emerging North-South axis of conflict), and next by the Reagan administration because of Carter's alleged neglect of a "window of vulnerability" (and his mishandling of the East-West axis of global confrontation with the Soviet Union). Yet, with the benefit of hindsight, we know now that it is the revised Nixon-Carter designs that started Reagan's endgame in the 1980s. For it is only after Nixon had resisted the nation's urge to come home that Carter could be an indispensable catalyst for the proud reaffirmation of "the decency and generosity and common sense" of our own people that inspired U.S. foreign policy.[18] And it is only after Carter had reaffirmed the relevance of American values in a skeptical world that Reagan could credibly attack the Soviet "evil system" as a "sad, bizarre chapter in human history whose last pages are even now being written."[19]

As shown during the Carter years, that commitment alone was not enough to force the pace of the Cold War and end it. From the start, therefore, Reagan's single-minded goal was not only to contain the Soviet Union but also to transcend communism and its state sponsor on the basis of a *complete* superiority that would be not only military but also ideological, economic, and societal. Instinctively, Reagan understood better than either of his two immediate predecessors that his first priority was not to rethink the world and its multilateral institutions, including the alliance system built by the United States during the previous three decades. Most urgently, Reagan assumed that for the world to regain trust in America and its leadership, the nation's self-confidence would have to be restored first. It's America, stupid: Reagan's immoderate optimism about U.S. power and values satisfied a national mood that had grown increasingly dissatisfied with, and resentful of, the drift of the previous years. This was Gaullism *à l'américaine*: inspired and led by an aging man who claimed to stand above party divisions despite his obvious partisanship, a dominant and self-assured America—Reagan's own version of de Gaulle's "princess in the fairy tales"—would end years of self-doubts and self-induced decline to put the world back in order.

The strategy thus defined by a seemingly disorderly mix of specific policies strengthened the president's unwavering optimism worked surprisingly well. In November 1984, Reagan's boast—"America is back"— was credible enough to give him an overwhelming victory over his

Democratic challenger; it was also sufficiently visible to discourage a Soviet leadership that no longer believed in overcoming the U.S.'s apparent ability to renew and expand its power nearly indefinitely. For notwithstanding the brutal recession of 1981–1982 and the tragedy of Lebanon in 1983–1984, the renewed vigor of the U.S. economy and the revitalization of its institutions had restored a coherent, vibrant, and convincing American model abroad—in sharp contrast with the inert, inept, and fractured Soviet system. Paradoxically, however, Reagan's approach worked perhaps too well—meaning too quickly to enable his administration to complete the new multilateralism promised by Kissinger and pursued by Zbigniew Brzezinski, his counterpart in the Carter administration, during the previous decade. But with mounting evidence of the Soviet collapse, none might be needed anyway as the Western democracies were rallying around a resurrected U.S. leadership, and a wave of democratic conservatism seemed to be sweeping the Third World. The Cold War was now about to be won. Victorious a third time in a century, America seemed to be losing a role in the world lest it be tempted to gain an empire.

What America lacked during the post-Vietnam half of the Cold War was not a new vision for world order. There was a vision, already stated, and there was an order, already tested—a vision and an order both based on the "self-evident truths" and "inalienable rights" of the American Republic, but which had remained broadly limited to the "half world" evoked earlier by Dean Acheson with primary reference to Europe. That most Western European nations and their citizens could now seek and achieve "life, liberty, and the pursuit of happiness" more openly, more widely, and more safely than ever before was not a small tribute to that vision. But enlarging the geographic scope of the democratic order—political unity, democratic freedoms, and regional security—thus achieved within the multilateral institutions inherited from the Cold War was not a modest ambition after the Cold War either. Until September 11, 2001, it seemed that such a vision could do, at least for a while.

COMMITMENT WITHOUT PURPOSE

After the Cold War, the absence of a definable common threat and the lack of a serious countervailing power left the alliance without a clear

purpose—meaning a new set of shared goals, and a common understanding of the adversary against which these goals might have to be
achieved. In January 1991, the first war against Iraq had lent some credibility to President Bush's claims of a "new international order" based on
the U.S. will to "retain the pre-eminent responsibility for addressing . . .
those wrongs which . . . could seriously unsettle international relations."[20]
That order would also grow out of the demonstrable evidence that even
in the absence of any pressing threat to the United States—reminiscent of
the postwar period before heavy bombers exposed U.S. territory to the
reach of any serious enemy—the United States would continue to provide
its allies with the security they might conceivably ensure at some point for
themselves, but not now and, in any case, neither as well nor as cheaply.
The U.S. ambition was daunting. It was not only driven by a desire to
preserve a status quo that favored the United States, but it also dared to
forsake it by speaking to the world the only language people understood—the language of democratic principles and values, punctuated by
the occasional use of force as and when needed to protect and promote
these principles.

The preponderance achieved during the previous decades left the
United States as the only country in the world with absolute sovereignty
and even a de facto right of interference that could be made absolute since
it could be asserted at will. That right, however, grew out of an obligation
imposed on the United States not only by the facts of its power, but also
from the abrogated claims of sovereignty made by states that did not respect the most elementary human rights to which the United States had
been committed since its birth. As the then-director of the Policy Planning Staff at the State Department, Richard Haass, put it, "Sovereignty
entails obligations. One is not to massacre your own people."[21] During
this unipolar moment, Cold War multilateralism thus faded, not because
it had failed but because it no longer seemed necessary or even relevant.
Taking its place at last was a new unilateralism that showed much of the
realism learned from the European allies during the Cold War, when
power often took precedence over justice, but with a restored streak of
old-fashioned Wilsonianism inherent to an American tradition that
sought justice ahead of power. In short, the United States would rely on
its superior capabilities, as well as on its reputation as a benign hegemonic

power, to supervise a new world order, herding its new friends in Eastern Europe into those institutions that had tamed allies and defeated adversaries, and keeping new rivals or enemies at bay, and regional and civil conflicts at a distance, whether by intimidation or persuasion.

At first, little of that resolve was shown during the years of indifference that surrounded the escalation of violence in the Balkans. In Bosnia, however, the criminals and their victims were known—flashes of earlier school days when "Sarajevo" was not a geographic site but a moment in history that was memorized as the catalyst for a horrific world war, and when camps designed for mass killing by Slobodan Milosevic brought back memories of horrific names, Auschwitz and all that, that can never be forgotten. Thus the ability to control ethnic violence in Bosnia and throughout the Balkans seriously tested what had been achieved during the previous forty years—not only whether it could endure, but also how. It is therefore in this small region that a resilient America and a renewed Europe would win or lose the post–Cold War peace, not because a supposedly "foreordained" war in the former Yugoslavia might once again explode into a world war, but because such a war, however limited it remained, would disrupt the transatlantic and intra-European structure built since World War II.

Whether the war in Bosnia was the "greatest collective failure of the West since the 1930s" can be debated, especially in light of the failures that followed elsewhere.[22] Unlike post-1919 Weimar Germany, post–Cold War Serbia could not be a catalyst for a general European conflict, if for no other reason than Europe (and, as was shown in Kosovo, the Serbs themselves) refused to be dragged into another continent-wide military conflict. Nor, unlike Germany during either world war, did Serbia's potential for war expand after the war had begun. By mid-1995, Milosevic's Serbs were already a spent force as the myth of their invincibility was exposed by Croatia's offensive, which the Clinton administration pointedly allowed to continue, and may even have encouraged, while it prepared to get a settlement for a unified Bosnia later that summer.[23]

Yet, Richard Holbrooke understood especially well (and earlier than most) the enormity of the issues at stake: not only to end the war and save Bosnia from Serbia but, and even more urgently, to save Europe and even the United States from themselves—the former's tragic history of bloody conflicts and the latter's foolish tradition of isolation and self-denial. For such goals to be achieved, NATO had to be preserved as America's prime institutional conduit to Europe, but it also had to be renewed as its members' security institution of choice. Otherwise, it threatened to be like a huge whale stranded on a beautiful Atlantic beach. If left untended, it would "die, stink, and pollute everything around it," within Europe because of the ensuing *sauve-qui-peut* among countries suddenly reminded of their past fears and conflicts, as well as with the United States, now denied its primary institutional point of entry into the continent.[24]

The Bush-Clinton reaction to the war in Bosnia hardly betrayed an imperial temperament. If there was only scant support for the use of U.S. force over an issue of indisputable moral significance and in a region of great importance because of its impact on U.S. interests in Europe, how could there be much support for a U.S. role elsewhere? With Americans watching the siege of Sarajevo on the evening newscasts after a plentiful dinner and with the discreet yawn that precedes a restful night, Bush *père* first, and Clinton next, proved to be equally indifferent during a presidential campaign that the former did not expect to lose and the latter was determined to win. In 1993, the incoming president not only seemed to lack interest in the world, he also lacked background. "At a time of crucial decisions" in Bosnia, it was deplored, "Clinton simply read the wrong book."[25] Buried memories remind of another president, Jimmy Carter, whose reaction to the Soviet invasion of Afghanistan had reportedly been to read a few books about an adversary whose action had "surprised" him; and lingering memories, too, recall pre-9/11 U.S. presidents whose first morning thoughts were more likely to evolve around domestic issues than around world events, except at a time of crisis.

Still, Bosnia reconfirmed not only the indispensability of American power but also the centrality of American leadership in post–Cold War Europe and, by implication, throughout the world. That status pointed to the reality of America as a nation like no other—namely, the sole remaining superpower, notwithstanding its explicit reluctance to commit its power to the purpose—the sense of mission—that had defined its rise to such a status in the world. Resisted by the first president Bush late during his administration, as well as by President Clinton during much of his first term in office, intervention in Bosnia was not the U.S. option of choice; rather it was imposed on the United States by Europe's failure to do more on its own, for lack of capabilities but also for lack of collective will. Even the coalition belatedly formed by the Clinton administration to negotiate the peace more than to wage a war was mostly designed to prevent the government in Belgrade from "playing off the Europeans against each other, or against us."[26] In Dayton, in the fall of 1995, Europe's presence looked like a courtesy extended by the United States to a few friends who wanted to look involved—part of a ritual embodied in a "contact group" that had been ambivalent about the use of military power, especially U.S. power, until it was reluctantly understood that worsening conditions on the ground left Europe with no better alternative. But that ambivalence was found among Americans too: everything else being equal, the war should have been left to the Europeans to win and to end. Exit strategies were therefore devised to reassure the U.S. Congress that Bosnia would not become another Vietnam but, notes Secretary of State Madeleine Albright, "it was soon evident [that these expectations] were utterly unrealistic."[27] Nor was it expected that the U.S. intervention, and the negotiations in Dayton, had settled anything, notwithstanding the risk that what was not negotiated in Dayton might be difficult to negotiate later.[28] The most immediate goal was to stop the war long enough—one year, or so it was pledged—to end it in some undefined way and at an ill-defined point in the future. (Later, in Kosovo, the immediate goal was to win the war—but not necessarily to end it in the absence of any specific plans for the Kosovars.)

If anything, Bosnia confirmed Europe's inability to offer an alternative to a leadership role that the United States seemed reluctant to exercise much longer. To repeat, the temptation for Americans was anything but imperial. Why not retire, or at least rethink the entangling relationships developed in earlier years? Why care about anarchy, whether in Europe or elsewhere, and why not enjoy the benefits of well-earned peace dividends? Answers should have been obvious. In 1945, the U.S. involvement in the world had not been a matter of vocation but one of position, which it also ceased to be in 1991 when order was no longer threatened by a hegemonic bid with a global reach (whether Germany or the Soviet Union in Europe, and Japan or China in Asia) or a regional bid with global consequences (like Iraq in the Persian Gulf). Now instead, the United States was simply too powerful to desist, as it used to do, or to remain aloof, as it used to prefer. Now instead, the U.S. involvement in the world responded to a range of interests much too significant to be viewed as anything less than vital, and much too important to be left dependent on the capabilities of allies, or the goodwill of adversaries.

In early 1991, the first draft of a grand strategy of protracted predominance was prepared for then-Defense Secretary Richard Cheney by then-Undersecretary Paul Wolfowitz, with leading contributions by many other analysts who later joined or sponsored the administration of Bush *fils*.[29] Although the first president Bush neither had the time nor the opportunity to enforce this global strategy, the 1991 Defense Policy Guidance (DPG) still read well ten years later, as it emphasized the two main interests of the new administration: to defend against the "proliferation of weapons of mass destruction and ballistic missiles, [and] threats to U.S. citizens from terrorism," and to protect U.S. "access to vital raw materials, primarily Persian Gulf oil" against "any hostile power."[30] Not surprisingly, the events of September 11, 2001, gave these interests and these threats an urgency they had lacked before, and proved to be the catalyst, or even the alibi, for an imperial zeal that had been absent after the collapse of the Soviet Union and the first Gulf War.

"The mission determines the coalition, and the coalition must not determine the mission," declared Defense Secretary Donald Rumsfeld in the fall of 2001, when announcing his intention to build a "coalition of coalitions."[31] More specifically, Rumsfeld's post-9/11 design suggested a pyramidal structure whose broad base of "willing" allies, not all of them but as many as possible, would narrow on its way up the pyramid, depending on the availability of capabilities relevant to the mission being confronted. That America would stand on top of such a structure—where the final relevance of willing and capable partners was to be determined—was a *droit de seigneur* for "a freedom-loving nation, a compassionate nation, a nation that understands the value of life," as Bush argued on October 11, 2001. But it was also a legitimate right of self-defense for a nation whose military capabilities permitted retaliatory or even preemptive action with or without any or most other countries. For a nation whose power was dominant before it had peaked, and could be endlessly renewed even after it had peaked—with projected defense spending of nearly $450 billion in 2005, more than $150 billion over spending levels at the close of the Clinton presidency—the only meaningful interventionist options left involved choices between various types of unilateralism—a continued willingness, that is, to act with other countries so long as they could follow U.S. leadership without delaying and complicating it, but also a renewed readiness to act alone otherwise.[32]

Whether this approach would be different from the past is a matter of degree only. Previously, the U.S. willingness to act multilaterally had always been selective because of a clear reluctance to accept significant constraints from the allies. In any case, in an alliance that was fundamentally unbalanced, a U.S. commitment to act multilaterally did not prevent unilateral decisions since the capabilities needed for the enforcement of such decisions would come mostly from one country anyway. On a few occasions, the United States refused to act because of the allies' reluctance to follow, as was the case, say, for President Eisenhower in Indochina in April 1954, when Britain refused to join the United States in a last-minute attempt to save the French in Indochina. But in this and a few other cases, such reluctance served as a convenient alibi for not doing what the United States was not eager to do anyway. In late 2001, Rumsfeld's "uni-multilateralism" kept the European allies generally underused during the war in Afghanistan, a recognized error that can be explained in part by the unusually urgent and the unexpectedly quick pace of the military campaign. That had not been the case for the Kosovo war, when the war had reaffirmed the need for NATO as the security institution of choice for its members and the many European countries that were seeking membership. But during the war in Afghanistan, European allies complained bitterly of the marginalization of an alliance that the United States praised for its willingness to embrace the mission, as decided by the United States, but which it found on the whole not sufficiently capable or relevant enough to wait to execute the mission.

For President Bush *fils*, letting go of NATO in 2002 was tempting. Why bother? The capabilities gap between America and its allies in Europe, already large throughout the Cold War, had been growing. Moreover, the transatlantic "power gap" now extended beyond the sole measurement of capabilities to cover widening differences over what these capabilities were—"hard" and "soft"—and how they should be used. Where Americans dialogued with power, as opposed to weakness, Europeans seemed more likely to dialogue with order, as opposed to force. Where Americans might insist on the need to *win* wars (militarily) before attending to their aftermath (political and otherwise), Europeans insisted on debating how to avoid a war, and if this could not be done, how to *end* a war even before demonstrating their commitment to fighting it.

Under such conditions, the NATO Summit that had been scheduled to take place in late 2002 for a so-called "big bang" enlargement of its membership threatened to be the end of NATO rather than its renewal. Not only was enlargement, the main achievement of the Clinton years, no longer enough to keep the alliance in business, it might force it out of business because of the organizational confusion and internal imbalances caused by the arrival of seven new members. Questions of capabilities and structures also needed to be addressed urgently—almost like the EU: enlarge in order to strengthen, but also strengthen in order to enlarge, and reform in order to do both. In November 2002 in Prague, therefore, Bush did not merely aim at completing the post–Cold War transformation started by its then-sixteen members in Rome in November 1991. He also started a new evolutionary process with a complete overhaul of the organization's capabilities and command structures—without which the alliance would lack the flexibility and the capability needed to plan and enforce a full range of global missions that would take NATO beyond its traditional purview in Europe.

There is some irony in this new start for NATO. In April 1949, the North Atlantic Treaty was not an American initiative, but it responded instead to repeated and even urgent European pleas for a credible and lasting commitment from the United States. The purpose of the alliance was readily identifiable: to contain the further spread of Soviet power and ideology, to prevent the revival of German hegemonic ambitions, and to keep American power committed to the security of Europe. These goals were all fulfilled because over the following years, an organization, NATO, was organized to serve a defense community built on increasingly converging interests and progressively compatible values between its members. Now, however, while confirming the U.S. primacy within NATO, and reasserting the centrality of NATO for its members' security, the 2002 Prague summit did not renew the alliance with a political consensus that could give NATO the mandate needed to make it usable. Or, to put it differently, granted that NATO was reinstated in Prague as the security organization of choice for all its members, there was no commitment from the alliance members to a common agenda in the post-9/11 security environment: allies must have a sense of what they might be called upon to do together, and of what they may be denied to do alone, if their alliance is to have any serious meaning for those countries it serves, as well as for those countries it might allegedly want to deter.

During the post-Vietnam half of the Cold War, various U.S. attempts to define a new multilateralism have exacerbated Europe's allegations about America's reliability—its isolationist instincts (extended to the world or, more narrowly, limited to a disengagement from Europe) or its unilateralist penchant (meaning a willingness to act outside a full NATO consensus). In turn, these concerns, found unwarranted and even abusive in the United States, have exacerbated America's own concerns about its allies' reliability—that is, their responsiveness to U.S. leadership and their ability to make effective contributions to the enforcement of that leadership. These terms define the rhetorical troika of transatlantic ambivalence—isolationism, unilateralism, and multilateralism. Depending on the issue at hand, every American has been, might be, or will become an "isolationist"—and every European will be, might become, or used to be fearful of America's "unilateralism" or "multilateralism." That dilemma—NATO's back, where is the alliance?—will have to be resolved for NATO to play effectively the global role to which it has been assigned since September 11.

A CHALLENGING AMERICA

"We are at war," George W. Bush told his vice president on September 11, 2001.[33] In the weeks and months that followed, the president's tone became increasingly confident and assertive—even, in the end, occasionally feverish and aggressive. In effect, the presidential leadership unveiled by Bush after these horrific events suited the nation's mood well, and probably better than would have been the case had his opponent been elected the previous fall in 2000 or, though less convincingly yet, four years later, in 2004. In an angry America, there was little room for equivocation; in a united and determined America, even the president's critics could be heard saying the words that had defined Barry Goldwater's failed presidential campaign in 1964—in your heart, you know he's right. "I got to know how I feel," the president was still insisting nearly three full years after September 2001, "to tell me what I think is the right way to act."[34]

The war started by these events also suited the president's temperament well and probably better, too, than would have been the case with the previous president. "I do not need to explain why I say things," later confided Bush. "That's the interesting thing about being the president. Maybe somebody needs to explain to me why they say something, but I don't feel like I owe anybody an explanation."[35] For a man who had shown a total lack of curiosity about the world in his youth as well as during his maturing political years, the world lost any mystery that might still interest the president after he witnessed these events. Now, Bush was satisfied with what he knew, and his beliefs narrowly shaped whatever else he remained willing to learn on the assumption that any new knowledge would serve to confirm and strengthen these beliefs.[36] Everything else would distract from the war at hand, and possibly compromise or delay its results—as would anyone who might have doubts about the war and the cause it served. In short, from that moment on, even a passing reference to "September 11" could serve as a credible explanation for every decision, every action—haunting memories that shortened policy debates because they introduced a clarity and even a certainty that demanded that the culprits and their associates be forcefully punished so that such attacks never be repeated. Faced with the question raised by Machiavelli's Prince—"What course will save the life and liberty of the country?"—Bush had but one single response: an unequivocal will to act with an unwavering sense of urgency. "I believe in results," asserted Bush.[37] And he added, in an aside seemingly aimed at other countries more than his own, "We're never going to get people all in agreement about force and the use of force. . . . But action—confident action that will yield positive results provides kind of a slipstream into which reluctant nations and leaders can get behind."

As Bush's former national security advisor, Condoleezza Rice was not expected to originate or debate ideas, and single out any particular view within his administration. Rather, her primary responsibility was to absorb all of the ideas, all equally plausible and all convincing in different measure, before compressing them in ways that would enable the president, in the words of one of her predecessors, "to perceive the essential among a mass of apparent facts" and "to impose some direction," meaning make decisions which Rice would then coordinate and implement.[38] "The key to asserting effective coordination," wrote Zbigniew Brzezinski, is "the right of direct access to the President, in writing, by telephone, or simply by walking into [the president's] office."[39] Because "coordination is predominance," and because Rice had "direct access at any time, not subject to anyone's control" more than any of her predecessors, including Kissinger and Brzezinski, her influence on the president, and her predominance over her peers was unequalled and unprecedented.

That Rice's views paralleled those of the president more closely than had ever been the case before did not serve the policy debate well during the first Bush administration. Like Bush, Rice believed that the direction best suited for the nation was one that combined power and morality.[40] Echoes of an American messianic tradition that was buried in the swamps of Vietnam, was heard during the Reagan years, was lost again in the back alleys of Mogadishu or the minefields of Kosovo, had now reemerged out of the ruins of the World Trade Center, or at the site of a crippled Pentagon. But echoes, too, of a presidential style and temperament drove the decision-making process largely on the basis of overpowering emotions and steadfast convictions rather than with powerful ideas and a stirring rhetoric. Rice shared and reinforced these traits, but she did not initiate or shape them. The attacks of September 11 did, not only for President Bush but also for her, not only as national security counselor, when she was the receptacle for contrary advice coming from Cabinet members, but now when, as secretary of state, she will be providing advice that her former deputy, Stephen Hadley, is bound to listen to attentively as the most reliable words he hears short of those coming from the president.

"He least likes me to say, 'This is complex'," Rice has said of "her" president.[41] In the United States, this approach to leadership sells well, and certainly better than in most European countries. A scholarly grasp of, or even interest in, world affairs is no prerequisite for presidential leadership in the world. Both Woodrow Wilson and Ronald Reagan managed a global war during its closing months and, for Wilson, in its immediate aftermath. The two wars were dramatically different, and so were the two men, but each was moved by a comparable commitment to the principles and values that had defined the rise of the American Republic and seemed to be threatened by an evil power. Determining which of the two presidents did better—the erudite professor of political science (and former president of Princeton University) or the "simplistic" movie actor—is not really difficult. In November 1918, Wilson sailed out of New York to Europe with "the best available experts, combed out of the universities and the government; crates of reference materials and special studies"—enough talent for a series of doctoral theses on the most effective ways to end the war that was expected to end all wars.[42] Yet, what soon followed Wilson's return were not post- but interwar years—a prelude to another world war that was fundamentally unavoidable because the peace Wilson helped negotiate at Versailles was on the whole neither acceptable to the defeated state nor satisfying to the victorious powers. By comparison, Reagan was no Wilson—except, perhaps, for the "passionate humanity" they both shared. He was a character with "a slabby, alabaster-like quality" that left his official biographer asking himself repeatedly (and skeptically), "How much does Dutch really know?"[43] Yet after this "banal" man had set the stage for a victorious and peaceful end to the Cold War came a full decade of postwar years that provided for a peace dividend that brought unprecedented affluence in America though, admittedly, no lasting order in the world.

Like President Bush since September 2001, every postwar president has faced a challenge he could call his own even though it was always imposed upon him by forces over which he rarely had much control. While the ability to meet that challenge was occasionally helped by an impressive intellectual pedigree (as was the case for John F. Kennedy during the Cuban missile crisis, but also Jimmy Carter during the Camp David negotiations), little education never was insurmountable (as proved to be the case for Truman, the architect of the postwar years). Not only Truman but also Nixon and Reagan (who attended second- and third-tier academic institutions) asserted the nation's leadership in the world boldly and, notwithstanding the criticism and apprehensions voiced abroad, they did so successfully. Indeed, how well mediocre students can do in public life is cause for wonder—the ultimate public form of anti-intellectualism in America. Dean Acheson, for example, found "studying hard at Yale . . . unnecessary" and his grades rarely rose above a C average.[44] That did not prevent him from becoming one of the nation's most successful secretaries of state—and that did not prevent the governor of Texas, another "C" student, from winning the highest political office in the land, long after he had forgotten the little he had learned at Yale and Harvard. In short, in the public view smarter is not necessarily better, as liberal democratic candidates have learned periodically from their more conservative opponents—the witty Adlai Stevenson, who was twice defeated by the bland Dwight D. Eisenhower; the intense Jimmy Carter, who could not keep up with Ronald Reagan; and the bookish Al Gore, who was rattled by George W. Bush's platitudes, which also derailed the intellectually complex John Kerry.

Europeans seem to hold different expectations for the leaders they elect, and usually celebrate after they have served. Imbued with the self-serving conviction that a well-educated and sophisticated elite produces better national and world leaders, and mostly unable to translate in their respective languages American phrases like "street smarts" or "horse sense," they reject many of the features that help elect a candidate in the United States as reflective of traditions that leave the nation unprepared for world leadership. Haunted by their own tragic history, they dismiss the U.S. penchant for "doctrines" and "visions" as oversimplifications of the complex realities their countries have lived and are still facing. "Regular" guys who go to Washington to defend the nation and its citizens are forgiven their rhetorical gaffes and their occasional ignorance or neglect of facts at home but not abroad. They appeal to a stand-up, action-oriented, idea-shy political culture that pleases the nation but few others. A leadership that reduces every issue to its essential core and combines all issues into an elusive doctrine works magically for local constituencies but plays poorly on the global stage. In early 2001, the caricature that had been drawn of Bush during the months preceding the election symbolized and confirmed everything that Europe liked least and feared most about America.[45]

That in the fall of 2000 most of the allies would have shown a preference for outgoing Vice President Gore was not unusual and, therefore,
should have remained without lasting consequence. A similar preference
emerged for the incumbent political party at the expense of Arkansas
Governor Bill Clinton in 1992, for then-Vice President Bush over Mass-
achusetts Governor Michael Dukakis in 1988, and for outgoing Presidents Ford and even Carter over then-Governors Carter in 1976 and
Reagan in 1980, respectively. As a result, Europe has never embraced a
newly elected president whose credentials—too old or too young, too
conservative or too liberal, too distant or too intrusive, and almost always
insufficiently prepared—have fallen seemingly short of European standards and expectations. In all instances, however, there was subsequently
a reversal of sort as facts and events overcame the campaign rhetoric and
forced him to become what he had pledged to not be during his rise to
power. In other words, with every new president comes a get-acquainted
period during which Americans should hear Europe's criticism of their
newly elected president with some indulgence, while Europeans should
appraise his action with some tolerance—more, at any rate, than is usually
shown on either side of the Atlantic.

Thus, in January 2001, Bill Clinton's popularity in Europe contrasted
sharply with the criticism that accompanied his first year in office, in
1993, when Europe had feared Clinton's "unilateral bullying" on trade
and other economic issues, his diplomatic faux pas in Bosnia and with
Russia, and his misuse of force in Haiti and Somalia—not to mention the
new president's apparent proclivity to pick fights with the main EU countries, including Britain (whose prime minister, John Major, had openly favored Bush's reelection) and Germany (whose economy was already
sputtering).[46] This bad start was eventually corrected, but Clinton's popularity in Europe at the close of his eight-year presidency was hardly justified by a legacy that was incomplete in the area of foreign policy. In the
Middle East, the Balkans, the Aegean, the Korean peninsula—as well as
with regard to defeated states (Russia), ascending powers (China), and
rogue states (Iraq), Clinton's goals proved all the more elusive as, for him
as well as for the nation the will was lacking, the commitments were ambivalent, and the interests were ill defined.[47] In January 2001, that legacy
of unfinished diplomatic and security business, combined with an unusually

chaotic transition period, therefore gave Bush a difficult start that, together with a wide range of unforced errors of his own making, worsened Europe's perceptions of his capacity for leadership.

Disrupted by the reminders of the president he replaced, and the agenda left behind, the Bush presidency was also hampered by ideological concerns that ended the third way favored by his predecessor and many of his European partners. That too, however, should not have been cause for lasting concern. Since 1945, the states of Europe have been usually more at ease with Democratic presidents (including John F. Kennedy and Bill Clinton, but not Jimmy Carter) than with Republican presidents (including Richard M. Nixon and Ronald Reagan but not Dwight D. Eisenhower) who carried with them, they feared, a heavy luggage of isolationism and protectionism. In this case, too, most of Europe has learned that these labels have not stuck, and that the republican rigidity they fear does not last longer than the democratic compassion they favor, as each Republican president, like his Democratic counterpart, uncovers opportunities that demand the sort of pragmatism to which they had initially objected. Nixon, who went to Peking to end the isolation of the People's Republic of China, and Reagan, who went to Moscow to end the Cold War with the evil Soviet Empire, are obvious examples. By the summer of 2001, this pattern seemed about to be confirmed again, as Bush's first two trips to Europe in June and July 2001—his first two such trips ever—were unusually successful and unveiled, according to then-EU Commissioner Chris Patten, a man who was "internationalist in outlook, open to dialogue, and ready to develop, not discard, America's relationship with Europe."[48] On the eve of September 11, 2001, Bush's standing in Europe was in fact likely to be above that of three of his four immediate predecessors at the same time in their respective presidencies—Clinton, Reagan, and Carter in 1993, 1981, and 1977, but not his own father in 1989.

As could be expected, the events of September 11 redirected the Bush transition, thereby causing the change that could have been anticipated relative to the positions articulated during the campaign, but causing it much earlier and in a different direction than should have been expected. Now, the president became much more demanding of his administration and his allies, and his timetable for action became less leisurely and, above all, less flexible. Up to then, Bush later acknowledged, he "didn't feel that sense of urgency and my blood was not nearly as boiling."[49] Although Europe rallied behind America to share its pain and horror, Bush's own relations with Europe were disrupted by his allies' ambivalence about him and their doubts about his decisions. This disruption was not about ideology but about a war that was widely denied beyond Afghanistan, even though it was broadly understood that the conflicts unveiled in New York could readily spread everywhere else. Faced with these conflicts, the meaning of America's leadership was also transformed, and doubts that had surfaced earlier about the experience of the new U.S. president and the ideology of his administration gained a new and more serious dimension.

Whether the Bush leadership can regain the allies' trust during his second presidential term is not clear. The opposition he faced from most of his counterparts in Europe and around the world, the public hostility, and even ridicule, to which he was exposed, will remain vivid for some time to come, notwithstanding a generally effective attempt at reconciliation in early 2005. In previous existential wars, or at times of especially dangerous crises, the U.S. leadership followed by the allies was assumed by presidents who already held the confidence of their allies abroad—Roosevelt on the beaches of Normandy in 1944, Kennedy in the Caribbean in 1962, and Bush *père* in the Persian Gulf in 1991. Truman did not enjoy such confidence, but he earned it after his electoral triumph in November 1948 gave him the time to carve his monumental place in European history as he put in place the structure within which the Cold War was waged and won on the basis of the ideas the U.S. president had developed with his European counterparts during his years in office. Had Truman lost the elections, his Republican opponent could not have ignored the Cold War, to be sure, but he would have approached it differently because the Truman legacy in late 1948 would have permitted him to develop a different structure—perhaps less reliant on alliances, less focused on Europe, less prudent when using force, and less flexible when dealing with adversaries. That was the stake of the 1948 presidential elections—not whether the Cold War would be waged but how. The way in which the war against terror will continue to be fought will also respond to unfolding events. Just like events modified Truman's thinking in 1950, conditions in Iraq or new attacks in the United States or among the European allies might also affect President Bush's thinking during his second term.

The decisive Cold War years began, therefore, with Truman's second term: by January 1953, the structure of the Cold War was sufficiently well in place not to permit much change during the following twenty years. So it was in January 1949, and so it is again in 2005, after another presidential election that will begin the decisive years of the war against terror. What is done during these years, how and how well, will also define the U.S. role in the world for the first half of the twenty-first century, as well as the kind of world in which that role will be played. For today's America and its president, there can no longer be isolation from, or moderation toward those forces that wish us ill. In a scared and scarred America, there is fire in the ashes, and the use of American force can either smother it or fan it to devastating flames, depending on how force is used, where and with whom. The most complex weapons designed to deter powerful enemies are now used for the most primitive ends: kill in order to not be killed, because the "Last Man, healthy, well fed, and pampered by technology" cannot afford to relinquish the future—his future—to the "First Man, condemned to a life that is poor, nasty, brutish, and short."[50] Europe's call for "the better America . . . liberal, outward-looking and generous" to return are likely, therefore, to fall on deaf ears in much of a country determined to show, in the words used by Bush but ready to be adopted by John Kerry had he been elected, that this is not an "impotent America . . . a flaccid, you know, kind of technologically competent but not very tough country . . . so materialistic . . . almost hedonistic . . . that we wouldn't fight back."[51] In 2005, America stands not only as a country challenged by its enemies, but also as a nation that is challenging its allies to stand up to their common adversaries. To that extent, the challenge faced by President Bush to earn the trust of his allies in order to build a Euro-Atlantic—Western—strategy to defeat the security conditions inherited since the end of the Cold War and the start of the wars of 9/11 parallels the challenge faced by President Truman immediately upon his election in November 1948.

Meanwhile, the defense of American policies need not be defensive. It is based on a record of genuine accomplishments. America is not a nation of passive and slightly embarrassed voyeurs.[52] It is an active and proud nation that has *earned* the right, deemed to be self-evident at the birth of the republic, to tell allies and friends what it is intent on doing in the world, and why. But that right is shared with allies and friends: When in doubt, over goals as well as over means, they, too, have gained the right to ask for explanations and provide alternatives before they choose to join or stand aside—though hopefully not in the way. It is when neither tells the other of its intentions or expectations, and when either acts without or in spite of the other, that the worst can be reliably feared, as was nearly the case in Bosnia in 1995 and as came to be the case over Iraq in 2003. For the West to act as one, it must acknowledge the divisions that prevail in its midst, between America and Europe and within Europe. For America to lead as one, it must end its own divisions, between those who still pursue the quixotic dream of leading by example only, thereby making of the nation's power and principles the exclusive conditions for order, and those who have concluded that the exercise of leadership is a realistic quest for enough followership to give that order the global endorsement it might lack otherwise.

4

A CHALLENGING
EUROPE

Because of commitments made by the EU heads of state and government—including especially a constitutional treaty signed in October 2004, and the opening of negotiations with Turkey agreed in December 2004—this is a challenging moment for Europe. Most broadly, this moment has to do with the final modalities of Europe's transformation from a mosaic of sovereign nation-states into an ill-defined union of member states. This transformation, which started as an extravagant dream after World War II, is now a reality that is grounded in the institutions that were built during the Cold War.

Historians will marvel. Burying the old Europe took too much time and too many lives; but giving birth to a new Europe was relatively quick and surprisingly civil. Nearly midway through the century, a "good" European like Stefan Zweig agonized, literally, over the many failed futures he had lived and no longer had the strength to endure. A full life later, remembering them and their tragic alternatives demands considerable imagination: fin de siècle Europe, vibrant and prosperous, ready to spread its dynamism and prosperity to others, on and beyond the continent, but mortally wounded by the war of 1914; postwar Europe, overwhelmed by the slaughters committed in its name during the war, but unable to bury them at last, before it became interwar Europe, seized by the tyrants, torn by its passions, betrayed by its intellectuals, and ready to fall again into the abyss that it had dug for itself.

"How many lives must I live," moaned Zweig after three decades of total wars had left him so hopeless as to drive him to suicide, away from a world that had already died thirty years earlier in 1914.[1] "We were born at the beginning of the First World War," wrote Albert Camus of his generation. "As adolescents we had the crisis of 1929; at twenty, Hitler. Then came the Ethiopian war, the civil war in Spain and Munich. These were the foundations of our education.... Born and bred in such a world, what did we believe in? Nothing."[2] But it is out of the ruins accumulated during such desolate life that the French humanist imagined a renaissance—the evocation of Sisyphus pursuing his mythical climb uphill because of his invincible hope that it would ultimately succeed, thus enabling him to die exhausted but happy. Admittedly, Europe still had its share of dying and killing during the second half of the century; entering a new century, however, Zweig, too, could have died happy because he could see that Europe's long and brutal struggle uphill has ended at last.

"Happiness" in this case does not mean a Europe whose "finality" produces a genuine and sovereign superstate, either as a matter of fact (territory, population, government, and army) or as a state of mind (loyalty, identity, values, and history). What is Europe, and what it must become, mainly raises questions of *modalité* rather than about its *finalité*. Yet if there is one conclusion that is so final as to be irreversible, it is that there is now in much of the continent a civilian space within which force can no longer be used by one state against another, or by any government over its people. For now at last, Europe can point to a Kantian, man-made miracle that has moved its once proud nations "beyond the Westphalian order into a postmodern supranational order."[3] For now at least, Europe can live a peace that is neither the imperial peace of the bully, nor the painful peace of the brave. Instead, the idea of Europe has permitted a peace of contentment and integration, which makes a return to past conflicts simply unthinkable because beyond imagination. Now instead, the risk is that the European peace has become so complete as to extend the denial of war within the boundaries of the EU into a rejection of war everywhere—a new European pacifism that would resist even good reasons for the EU and its members to wage war against genuine threats to their security and institutions. That, too, is a significant dimension of Europe's current defining moment, and another aspect of the transatlantic debate early in the twenty-first century.

As a rising power in the world, the Union formed by the countries of Europe has interests that are global in scope and vital in significance as the EU renews and expands its spheres of influence and values beyond the realm of its members' former empires. That influence is enhanced by a reputation that the states of Europe have renewed over the past fifty years, when other regions in the world found the lessons they taught worthy of emulation: that history can be made to change its course, away from war, and that geography can be helped to change its ways, without war. Europe's appeal does not merely spring from the advantages of an unfinished single market standing and growing next to large underdeveloped areas in the East and the South. All together rather than one at a time, the states of Europe rely on capabilities that include preventive security tools like trade policy, economic aid, and public diplomacy that are competitive with those available to the United States. Admittedly, military capabilities and political unity are lacking, but the next few years will show whether Europe and its Union can also acquire the former and achieve the latter if it is to move up to the next level: as a power in the world that can also stand as a world power, together with, rather than separate from, its vital partner across the Atlantic—a transatlantic superpower but not a European superstate.

NATION-STATES AND MEMBER STATES

To understand, wrote Isaiah Berlin, "is to perceive patterns."[4] Patterns are not shaped by theory but proposed by history as a succession of "accidents" whose origins are often untraceable and whose consequences are often unintended. The pattern that has grown out of Europe's history over the past fifty years is seductive. With nation-states reinventing themselves as member states of the Union they form or which they hope to join, Europe is achieving a new *synthesis* that is making it whole at last.[5]

The decisions to come, which form an endgame loosely dubbed as "finality," are a challenge for the states of Europe but they are also challenging for the United States, their most intimate partner.[6] Criticism and even resentment of European allies and their policies should not stand in the way of genuine admiration for the achievements of the European countries and their statesmen. This is Europe's third territorial revolution in half a millennium: past the long-forgotten city-states, beyond the worn-out nation-states, and onward to a new territorial breed known as member states. Even as that revolution unfolds, Europe's nation-states can be remembered with some emotion. These were "sublimated individuals" whose personality and character were shaped by the idea citizens had of their history and traditions.[7] The greatness produced by each nation-state in Europe was but one small fraction of the greatness produced by all of Europe—the literature, the music, the painting, the architecture, and much more.[8] The beauty found in every part of Europe is but a limited part of the beauty uncovered throughout the continent—the landscapes, the peoples, the designs, the cuisines, the languages, and more.

These memories are perpetually renewed because, even in this moment of finality for Europe, they help sustain the emotional pride in the nation, and the sense of personal loss associated with the erosion of the ideas it carried.[9] The "princess" imagined in de Gaulle's "fairy tale" and narrated in his postwar memoirs was specifically French, like the "certain idea" de Gaulle had of his nation, but there were other princesses, other tales, and other ideas imagined elsewhere with comparable love and passion. Every one of these princesses now holds or embodies "a certain idea" of Europe and its institutions rather than an idea of the nation and its history. What happened to the "civilizing mission" and what became of the "white man's burden" formerly revered as a central part of Europe's history? Now that history is found elsewhere: past Britain, France, Germany, or any other part of the Old World, it is reconstructed instead around the more recent history of an American presence that Europeans seem to resent, welcome, resist, and invite altogether. As old Europe is *passé*, will America be its future? In the new Europe, that question alone would suffice to create much anguish and some indignation. But there is more (or worse): to avoid drifting into a numbing Euro-Atlantic oneness, the most distinctive European flavor seems to come mainly from the defunct empires that exert their new influence through the ever larger immigrant communities they have brought into each of yesteryear's "mother countries." Which is it—or rather, which does it threaten to be:

the return of the empires to Europe from across the Mediterranean, or its drift into the realm of the new imperial power across the Atlantic?

The cumulative consequences of Europe's transformation on its citizens have become causes for public concern. After 1945, when a handful of European countries began to explore the terra incognita of European integration, the future was not a pressing issue. Rather, these countries were motivated by a widespread fear that the political divisions they had known in the past would perpetuate, and ultimately renew, wars in Europe. In other words, the new Europe was not born out of a single, or even common, vision of the future. Instead, it is the shared vision of a failed past that served as a flashlight for illuminating a dark present of ruins and shame. Nor was there any attempt to anticipate the end point to which the process might lead, beyond meaningless abstractions that originated in French but usually lacked equivalents in other European languages—*Europe des nations*, *Europe des états*. Instead, an elusive institutional logic defined an ever more cumbersome discipline that seemed to unfold, mechanically at first, and state-driven next: deepen in order to widen, widen in order to deepen, and reform in order to do both.

Now, however, the evidence of EU constraints on its members' sovereignty and the intrusiveness of its bureaucracy in the day-to-day lives of its citizens are producing more of a public debate over what has been, and is being done in the name of Europe. Granted that the Union gives its members a size and even an identity without which none might otherwise be able to survive, what can each of them keep as its historically sovereign domain—who does what, and why? Debating that question in an ever larger union also threatens to restore a hierarchy among member states led by a select core group of "pioneer states" favored by French president Jacques Chirac—who does what and why, to be sure, but with or without whom?

This, however, is not a transatlantic debate but a debate within Europe with possible—indeed, likely—consequences on its relations with the United States, including U.S.-EU and EU-NATO relations. What is Europe, and what does it stand for, or against? The question that follows is equally daunting: what and who is "we"—who is (meaning who is in) Europe, and who is not? However phrased, this question starts with the many definitions of what Europe used to be, the enlightened nation-states that produced the Age of Reason and all that, but also a killing field that produced the Age of Empires and the total wars of the twentieth century. It is that history that still stands in the way of finality—a European union of member states that overcome their national differences to act as the power in the world it has become again, even if it cannot stand alone as the world power it has ceased to be.

Some countries in Europe still struggle to assert their national identity within Europe, and Europe's regional distinctiveness relative to the rest of the world—an institutional third way "between the extreme individualism of America and the extreme collectivism of Asia."[10] This is not an easy struggle, however, least of all for the newer EU members who were not there, "at the creation," during the Cold War, or whose sovereignty was only restored a decade ago after the Cold War. The latter especially are where France used to be ten years after the Rome Treaties had been signed—when de Gaulle, for example, used to boast of a "France that cannot be France without grandeur." More modest French claims for a "France that cannot be France without Europe," as President Mitterrand liked to say, came later, with a passion that was shared by his counterpart in Germany, Helmut Kohl (and silently echoed or acknowledged elsewhere). Could it be, however, that the compelling trends that conditioned the rise of Europe throughout the Cold War, from the top down, might now be reversed, and that the Union painstakingly organized over the past decades could now be at risk, from the bottom up? Too much stress on the institutions, too many crises between their members, and too many demands on their citizens make the growing public ambivalence understandable.[11] Europe is "an exercise in institutional creativity" that is not readily comprehensible.[12] The plea to become something more, meaning "European," can be heard more easily when that something remains unstated and elusive; for most people, however, it is harder to hear a plea to become something else, especially as that "thing" called Europe becomes so big as to be progressively unrecognizable—or so recognizable (meaning American) as to cease to be acceptable. The paradox, then, is that Europe can be "Europe" only by being less European and becoming instead more American—or, at least, more like "a certain idea" of the United States of America.[13] Thus would close the circle that started in the eighteenth century when Europe was left behind as the central part of America's past, and would now end with America as a defining model for Europe's future.

The experience is odd and somewhat schizoid.[14] Even while Europeans become more American each day, they spend more time looking for ways to complain about America for what it does, and Americans for what they are. But even these complaints cannot prevent a cultural assimilation across the Atlantic. For what Europeans bemoan is a fading idea of America which is being challenged no less than their memories of a fading Europe: America reminds Europe of the dark angels of its own past, and Europe introduces America to the somber demons of its own future. "Are there common experiences and traditions that are the basis in every European citizen of an awareness of a political destiny which we have experienced together and which we could fashion in the future?" ask two of Europe's leading philosophers, Jurgen Habermas and Jacques Derrida, when reflecting about the "political profile" of Europe for the new century.[15] Their point is to argue on behalf of a Europe that cannot be Europe without more distance from America—meaning unless it does a great deal of cultural cleansing that would free the Europeans from the alleged pollution that has drifted across the Atlantic over the years. Paradoxically, however, the European profile they draw points to the idea that America still has of itself: the embodiment of a "civilizing process" that pursues "an ethos of solidarity seeking equal rights for all" on behalf of a "Kantian belief in a global domestic politics" and a collective "will [to] correct the failings of the market."

Many, if not most Americans measure poorly the reality and the magnitude of Europe's transformation to date. Instead of applause over how far Europe has come, there is too much moaning over how far it still needs to go. Would that be otherwise, there would be justification for much satisfaction. The integration of Europe is a European idea that only American power and leadership could help launch over fifty years ago, and have actively helped succeed since. An "American view of European union" presented a few years after 1945 already described U.S. policy in Europe as having "gone far toward committing the United States to the establishment of a European Union of some kind," and found "nothing . . . more timely and reasonable than a convention . . . to form a more perfect union of the European states."[16] But the idea of a European Union is also, in a deeper sense, an American idea because this is, after all, the idea that shaped the birth of the American Republic. At last, Europeans are doing in their own habitat what so many other Europeans did on American soil over two hundred years ago. To be sure, the calendar is not the same. What was born in 1776 was "not the infant nation, but the embryo: or rather, the nation was born so premature that for the next ninety years it existed only as a potentiality."[17] But the overall goal, which aims at a consolidation of an ill-defined territorial space—geographic, political, religious, or cultural—is similar.[18] In some strange way, the history of European union stands today past the Articles of Confederation but, on the eve of a politically difficult debate over its constitutional treaty, before the federal constitution framed a decade later; past the Civil War but, faced with unresolved questions over the treatment of its Muslim minorities, before the civil rights debate waged and won a century later; and, as it contemplates further enlargement in Turkey and elsewhere, in step with the protracted cultural debates that defined the final enlargement of the American union, from Utah in 1896 to New Mexico fifteen years later.[19]

It is not surprising that new obstacles would be emerging at this late date. To acknowledge them is not to denigrate Europe's ability to overcome them. To ratify a constitution? To welcome Islam? To build a common army? The decisions ahead are daunting. What began after 1945 as a mere time-out from European history—a reprieve from wars and conflicts—has evolved into something permanent: the end of a prolonged moment in Europe's history. What, exactly, is the political "finality" of that community; what are the institutional modalities of this union?[20] A public malaise about the Union and its future was apparent before the constitutional treaty gave it a focus that had been lacking before, even during the difficult debate over the launch of a single currency ten years earlier. To influence this debate—which is a debate over EU membership—Europe's leaders are mostly weak and permissive, driven for the most part by short-term political rivalries and ambitions that compare poorly with their predecessors' visionary convictions. Theirs is also a political "third way" that no longer shows the urgency that used to add passion to their discourse. "Why am I expected to be of the same opinion today as I was six weeks ago?" asked one of Stendhal's main characters about his future.[21] "That would mean I was the slave of my opinion." Ideological slavery is hardly the fate of Europe's new ruling class whose postmodernist approach to political accountability transforms reality into what it is said to be rather than what it is. Thus, with an implicit recognition that there may be no alternative to the policies in place, dissent is a path to political power built with rhetorical bricks and charismatic cement.

The only thing that is real is the confusion thus created. For what does it mean for a political leader in Europe to boast about "the economy doing better" or "well"— relative to what, to whom, and to when? These judgments readily stand in the way of changes that are deemed to be unnecessary, premature, or late depending on whether the going is said to be good or bad. When a stalemate emerges, values and principles and morality and all the other features of the way we were become easy substitutes for real policy choices. European leaders and their critics can thus show a feel-good conscience that contrasts with the do-nothing institutions they ignore or the read-my-lips political opponents they hope to mute. Single-minded ambitions rule over convictions that are kept conveniently flexible: political leaders who stand tall relative to their opponents can stand for little while they echo the voices of distant but much-admired political ancestors to explain their choices in eloquent Churchillian tones or with convincing Gaullist appeals. In this political environment, Europe and its institutions are or may become a ready-made alibi for each national setback and every domestic pain. In the midst of Europe's attempt at adopting the modalities that will define its finality, neither the fading idea of the nation-state nor the intrusive institutions to which they have abandoned much of their sovereignty are ideas worth suffering and even voting for—unless even that finality is explained as a need to counter or balance the senior partner across the Atlantic or the rising threat across the Mediterranean.

"I was turned out," complained Margaret Thatcher in June 1995, "because I said No to Europe, No, no, no."[22] Whether that claim is true is open to question. In the 1980s, Thatcher never truly said no; she merely meant to say not now. In coming years, however, political risks could grow out of a repeated "Yes to Europe, Yes, yes, yes"—unless "Europe" itself is used as a populist alternative to America, thus making of its institutions an anti-American tool that would be promptly abandoned by those EU members that refuse to adopt an allegedly multipolar vision of the future aimed at the United States.

These are not happy prospects. With already twenty-five members on board, an ever larger Union may no longer be necessarily better, but a Union made smaller by the withdrawal of some of its current members would certainly be worse; and an ever closer Union may no longer be more efficient for all its members, but more than one union—two or even three, each smaller and all moving at their own separate speeds—is likely to be much worse. The states of Europe can no longer pursue effective national policies separately, not only because they are individually too small but also because they no longer have separate control of the instruments needed for the execution of these policies. Nor are smaller European groupings likely to work better than the last time they were tried, which is when, against U.S. wishes, Britain formed a European Free Trade Association (EFTA) that attempted to outdo or outbid the European Economic Community. That hardly worked then, especially for the less ambitious EFTA group, and it cannot be expected to work much better now.[23] In the absence of any viable or preferable alternative, what ought to concern the United States most is not whether further advances are desirable, but whether anything can be done to influence Europe's choices in ways that reinforce past achievements—or at least avoid making these choices even more difficult because of U.S. opposition.

Preference for a larger Europe has been a constant feature of the U.S. interest in, and commitment to, a united Europe: more than two partners when Britain and France signed the anti-German Treaty of Dunkirk in 1946; more than five, when the Brussels Pact established the Western European Union (WEU) in 1948; more than six to make room for Britain when the European Defense Community (EDC) was proposed in 1950.[24] It remained true after the Rome Treaties were signed in 1957, and for the balance of the Cold War the United States always had a favorite candidate that would complete Europe's geopolitical contour—into the Atlantic with Great Britain in 1973, into the Aegean and nearer the Balkans with Greece in 1981, deeper into the Mediterranean with Spain and Portugal in 1986, and up to the North Sea and away from neutralism with Sweden and Finland (as well as Austria) in 1995—as if the best in the West was always expected to lie in the "new" Europe found at the ever expanding periphery of the hard European core represented by France and Germany.

Initially, the U.S. interest in enlargement satisfied a convincing Cold War logic: widening the area of affluence and stability in Europe reinforced and expanded the U.S.-sponsored zone of influence and security in the West. As European institutions grew, a centrist political stability settled and prosperity spread throughout—in France, Germany, and Italy first, and next in Ireland, Greece, Spain, and Portugal. Even more importantly, these gains defined a civilian space within which wars ceased to be thinkable. In short, an ever closer and ever larger Europe helped contain Soviet power and ideology, but it also helped America feel increasingly at ease—and even at home—with a democratic Europe and in a cohesive West. At the end of the Cold War, all twelve members of the European Community (except Ireland) were also NATO members, and only three of the fourteen European NATO members (Iceland, Norway, and Turkey) were not EC members.

After the Cold War, the Clinton administration confirmed the logic of expansion—bigger is better—and quickly pushed for the eastward enlargement of the main Euro-Atlantic institutions. That, too, was not a matter of false sentimentalism. Rather, it had to do with concerns that failure to associate the former adversaries to the benefits associated with the EU and NATO might perpetuate instabilities inherited not only from the Cold War but also from all the European wars that had preceded it. But enlargement would also renew and strengthen the Atlantic faith of the West by bringing into the alliance and the Union countries whose recent experiences had left explicitly sensitive to, and grateful for, U.S. leadership and values. To this extent, it is in this "new" Europe that would now be found the best of the West, and it is there, too, that the EU would be asked to assume a full share of Europe's postwar reconstruction and rehabilitation from the wars of the twentieth century in the East, as well as an appropriate share for the management and settlement of the conflicts of the twenty-first century in the South. The converging parallelism of EU and NATO enlargement was confirmed in May 2004, when the EU welcomed ten new members, including eight that had already joined NATO either the month before, in April 2004, or four years earlier, in April 1999. The two processes moved even closer as the EU was making plans to welcome three more NATO countries—not only Bulgaria and Romania, but also, at last, Turkey, the only European NATO member denied EU membership against its will.

THE DARKER SIDE OF THE UNION

Heard in the context of Europe's quest for a new identity, the questions raised by the growing presence of Islam are fraught with consequences, not only within the EU but also for the EU role in the world, including its relations with the United States. Transatlantic perspectives on Europe and its future predictably differ. When the EU looks across the European continent, its expansion is largely geographic; when the EU members look across the Mediterranean, their thinking is mainly cultural; and where the United States pleads for a transformation of the Muslim world as a primary foreign policy issue, the EU countries hope for the transformation of their Muslim communities as a domestic issue.

Europe and Islam still view themselves away from (or even in opposition to) each other more often than in association with one another. Each commonly defines its identity and affirms its specificity in order to escape the other's—"foreign, different, if not barbarian, fundamentalist or fanatic" are words used to describe Europe's worst vision of Islam but also Islam's worst vision of Europe and the West.[25] There may be some debate over where enlargement ends in the East, but there is little debate over where it ends in the South, notwithstanding a Muslim presence that makes of Islam the second most populous religion within the EU and nearly each of its members.[26] The irony is for every European to see and for many of them to fear: even while millions of Muslims in Europe fail to be fully integrated as European Muslims, Europe, which used to aim at regaining its past credentials as a respected power in the Middle East, is taking the allure of a Middle Eastern power.[27] The questions asked about the presence of Islam *in* Europe—within each of its nation-states and as one of its member states—now surpass in intensity and significance questions formerly raised by an evolving relationship between Islam *and* Europe.

All over Europe, citizens of any faith struggle to respond to a collective European discipline that demands their individual allegiance. But, an added burden, Muslims in Europe who struggle to become European Muslims also resist the need to surrender their religious authenticity to a state that imposes its own secular discipline upon them. All too often subjected to rampant discrimination, denied equal access to opportunities within the law, and seething over the neglect of their cultural needs, Muslim citizens become increasingly sensitive to readily available religious symbols and slogans for mobilization against the collective humiliation they endure and for the communal pride they feel. Resentful of their political and societal isolation, they become dependent on former home countries for spiritual comfort and escape from the aberrant rigidity of their adopted lands. In short, the potential for a future radicalization of Islam in Europe is emerging deep into the "Arab streets" of EU members where there is mounting evidence of a renewed interest in an ethnic identity of a kind that goes beyond the demands for "ghetto rights" that characterized the civil rights movement in the United States half a century ago.[28] Taking the form of Islamic fundamentalism, and aimed at replacing the host country's secularity with a divine societal order for its communities, that identity could find its expression in bursts of terror organized by a few extremists against U.S. targets in Europe; but they could also be unleashed more spontaneously against targets in Europe with a significant cultural meaning for the Europeans themselves. As was the case during much of the Cold War, when large "foreign national (communist) parties" influenced the security debate in Europe and with the United States, the war on terror is raising the specter of "foreign national forces" whose impact because of a few extremists would undermine the totality of the security debate within Europe, as well as between Europe and the United States.

Europe's vulnerability to acts of terror was real even before September 11, 2001; the only question was when. After Madrid was attacked on March 11, 2004, the question became where else, as well as how and how often: beyond subsequent attacks in Turkey, the Netherlands, and Russia later in 2004, other such attacks in 2005 can target a nearly infinite range of soft targets, and rely on an abundance of local extremists whose numbers are likely to grow as their anger deepens. Because the United States, the wars of 9/11 in Iraq and elsewhere, and even the Arab-Israeli war are only a small part of that anger, with the brunt of that anger more specifically focused on local conditions, national policies that engage Islam abroad while refusing to integrate it at home are not sufficient for protection.

Public apprehensions that the integration of Islam in Europe might be conducive to an Islamic Europe are strengthened by demographic changes in all EU countries, combined with immigration flows from North Africa and other countries south of the Mediterranean. Even though the total population in EU-25 will remain fairly constant over the next fifteen years, it is expected to decline steadily after 2020, slowly at first and faster later—especially in Italy, Spain, and Germany (with small increases projected in France, Ireland, Luxembourg, and Great Britain). Nor is that all. Even as Europe becomes smaller, it is also projected to become older as longer life expectancy brings the number of elderly persons in EU-15 (aged sixty-five and over) from 61 million in 2000 to 103 million in 2050, while the number of young persons (under the age of fourteen) falls from 69 million to 58 million.[29]

These trends—fewer young people to replenish a dwindlling labor force, and more senior citizens to deplete the social security coffers—may deny Europe the workforce needed to remain competitive. The average age in EU-15 is about thirty-eight years, about the same as in the United States. That average is expected to remain steady (and even recede slightly) in America, but it is projected to exceed fifty-three years in Europe in 2050, by which time EU-15 would have a working-age population estimated at 201 million in 2050, a fall of nearly one-fifth relative to 2000. Indeed, while Europe was dreaming of a high-tech future that used to be most closely associated with California, their citizens were launching a gray age that Americans associate most commonly with Florida. These trends are not affected by enlargement as demographic conditions in all ten new EU members closely parallel trends in Europe, especially with regard to the average fertility rate that barely exceeds that of EU-15.

The lack of labor mobility is also a significant factor in assessing Europe's response to these demographic changes. Unlike the United States, a widespread reluctance to go where the EU job supply is highest and most rewarding is not a matter of regulations but one of traditions and languages. Only 225,000 people, or 0.1 percent of the total EU population, changed their official residence between two countries in 2000. Nor is there much job mobility within each country or in each city: in 1999, about one worker in nine had been with the same employer for less than one year, as compared to 30 percent in the United States.[30] Even with a fuller use of employable labor and improved productivity, these demographic trends point to the need for more foreign labor. Indeed, the United Nations estimates that the EU countries will need between 47 and 79 million immigrants during the first half of this century. Even if birth rates were to pick up again, a longer life expectancy will keep the ratio of working people very low relative to the population as a whole: from 2000 to 2030, the size of the labor force in EU-15 is expected to decline by 9.2 percent, while the old age dependency ratio is expected to increase to 104.3 percent.

Moreover, life expectancy is likely to rise more and faster than currently anticipated, as the benefits of an unfolding "revolution in medical care" (RMC) reach the populace during the next decade, both as a matter of science and as a matter of social policy. Already, base-line projections of very-old-age dependency ratios in EU-15 (aged eighty-five or over, as a percentage of those aged twenty to sixty-four) are estimated to increase from over 3 percent in 2000 to 10 percent in 2050. Neither the pace nor the costs of an RMC can be measured with much reliability, but historical precedents serve as reminders that even under more benign circumstances, health services have grown faster than prices in the general economy.

Admittedly, the countries of Europe have endured many demographic crises since the phenomenal era of population growth in the nineteenth century, when Europe's population grew from one-fifth to one-fourth of the world's population, even though about 40 million Europeans left the Old World to build a better life elsewhere.[31] Even after 1945, when Europeans gave up on war, birth rates stayed low—barely balanced by the "return of the empires" to the colonizing countries. But entering the twenty-first century, with deaths expected to exceed births by 14 million people from the 1990s to the 2020s, and without any expectation that the EU could return to self-renewal levels of about two children per woman before the mid-2020s at the earliest, Europe is bound to become smaller and older unless it becomes more racially diverse, which the countries of Europe do not seem prepared to do for the time being.

Such conditions affect Europe's security, broadly defined, in several ways, and they also impact the totality of its relations with the United States. First, the rise in old-age dependency causes additional budget expenditures for rising pension and health costs, which will be enormously difficult to sustain without growth levels that have been beyond Europe's reach for the past decade. To make matters worse for harassed politicians, the budgetary constraints imposed by the Growth and Stability Pact increases competition for finite budgetary funds between what the state must do to improve public welfare on the one hand, and what must be done for the nation's security on the other. Changes in the criteria set by the pact would not significantly modify this competition for funds, which is complicated further by a "revolution in military affairs" that increases defense spending for equipment and training no less substantially than, and as quickly as, increases in medical costs for the elderly. Lacking such funds, Europe will find it difficult to manage its civil order from within, while attending to the costs of it proves unlikely to maintaining security in and outside its collective borders.

Second, and impacting further Europe's ability to produce military power, a shrinking pool of young people reduces the availability of military personnel, but it also reduces the family's patriotic willingness to sacrifice its single child on behalf of the nation or in the name of multilateral institutions—whether the EU, NATO, or the UN. In other words, Europe's ability to produce and use military capabilities will continue to decline on the combined grounds of priorities, resources, and will. Third, local population dynamics may create conditions for less political stability and more political extremism. That would be especially evident under conditions of growing terror anywhere in Europe, as an increasingly emotional reaction to such conditions would progressively spill over and intensify from one EU country to another. Even outside of the security conditions associated to the wars of September 11, different fertility rates between distinct ethnic groups that maintain adversarial relations create imbalances (and, on occasion, instabilities) that exacerbate public perceptions of, and reactions to, allegedly "massive" immigration. This condition is especially significant for multiparty political systems where community-based votes can achieve minority-induced political control of the fragmented majority. Finally, dissymmetrical demographic trends between the United States and the states of Europe widen the gap between them as America contemplates a European partner that suffers from a shrinking economic market hampered by an uncompetitive labor force, changing societies that respond to different foreign policy and security priorities, and a dwindling capacity for the production of soft power and the use of military power.[32]

After its enlargement to 75 million more people located in eight countries in the East, plus Malta and Cyprus, but prior to its expected enlargement to another 100 million people or more, including Bulgaria and Romania in 2007, as well as Turkey and others several years later, Europe is losing the sense of community that had deepened while its membership expanded from the original six to fifteen members. Whether bigger is actually better is now bitterly questioned by old and new members alike, as the states of Europe struggle over what the institutions to which they belong can and ought to do—how and when—in order to better serve their expanding community—where and why. In early 2005, the EU and its members (still standing as nation-states) proceed as if each mattered more than the other—each nation-state relative to its partners, and all nation-states relative to the institutions. The concept of "as if" is troubling: the grandchildren of Europeans who refused "to die for Danzig" sixty years ago resist exaggerated prospects that they may be asked to starve for their new commercial partners in Frankfurt, suffer for their new brothers in Warsaw or Madrid, or convert for their new home in Brussels. To view a return to the nation-state as if it were representative of all the citizens' wants and receptive to all of their needs is "a subjective, idealistic self-definition in which the idea takes absolute precedence over reality and consciousness determines being."[33] The nation's sovereign reality is foreclosed in the institutional cage in which the state's representatives are locked, and from which their ability to respond to the wants and needs of their constituencies is questioned. In other words, cease to tell the nation-states what they can do for the institutions to which they belong, but have the institutions tell the member states what they can do for them. Lest that be the case, mainly managed from the top down, the European institutions could face a serious crisis of legitimacy, from the bottom up.

As a candidate for EU membership that embodies what Europeans fear most and like best about Europe and its Union, Turkey stands at the center of this crisis. The geopolitical case for bringing this NATO country into the EU by a certain date is compelling. As President Bush forcefully declared at the NATO summit in June 2004, "Including Turkey in the EU would prove that Europe is not the exclusive club of a single religion . . . [and] would also be a crucial advance in relations between the Muslim world and the West."[34] But Europe's ambivalence about Turkey's membership is not just a geopolitical issue; rather, it is one of cultural juxtaposition and societal conformity. That ambivalence finds its roots in an earlier time, when Europe made room for one faith only, which was the Christian faith. While Europe's view of Islam as a "heresy" has evolved, the core belief that it should be kept at a distance has not fully disappeared.[35] For the United States to ignore these concerns and attempt to hurry the EU's timetable raises unwarranted expectations and can even harden resistance among some current EU members. No less significantly, U.S. insistence can also open new fault lines within NATO, thereby complicating other decisions that involve important U.S. interests—as happened in early 2003 when Belgium and France denied the use of NATO assets to protect Turkey prior to the war in Iraq, and as happened again at the NATO summit in Istanbul in June 2004 with President Chirac's blunt objections to his U.S. counterpart's insistence that "as a European power" Turkey "ought to be given a date . . . for eventual acceptance" in the European Union.

The complexities of EU enlargement, especially its cultural dimensions, should be readily understandable for an American union whose own expansion was often complicated by demands that applicant territories first adopt political, economic, and social institutions that matched those found in the Union. Thus, it took half a century and seven applications for membership before the people of Utah gained statehood in January 1896—after they had agreed to back away from a holistic view of religion that made of polygamy a divinely instituted obligation among its most faithful adherents. The cultural clash was openly discussed: "For Mormons, polygamy represented holiness and godliness, but it was a symbol of deviance and debauchery for Protestants and Catholics."[36] New Mexico, too, took more than sixty years before it moved beyond its territorial status and joined the Union in 1911. Throughout that period, statehood was opposed because New Mexico's predominantly Indian and Hispanic population was deemed too foreign and too Catholic for admission in the American union. For Colorado, statehood came faster, but not without equally angry and lengthy debates in congress over "roving, unsettled horde[s] of adventurers" who "are in Colorado solely because a state of semi-barbarism prevalent in that wild country suits their vagrant habits."[37]

The appeal of the EU is a tribute to its achievements, but there is growing concern that more enlargement of its membership may compromise, or at least weaken, the degree of integration already achieved not only within the EU but also in each member state. Within the EU, new members challenge the capacity of its institutions, originally conceived for a much smaller and more homogenous community, to perform coherently. In turn, the reform of these institutions, which takes the form of a constitutional treaty, is challenging the members' willingness to accept more erosion of their sovereignty even as they lose more of their influence on institutional decisions of growing importance. Within each member state, new immigrants are also challenging the ability of the state to attend to their needs and ensure full acceptance by the local communities they have chosen to adopt. In each case—the collective integration of the Union, as well as the integration of each of the national communities that populate the Union—the logic of integration clashes with the logic of assimilation: the difference, that is, between becoming something more, which most citizens will accept, if deemed beneficial, and becoming something else, against which most people will rebel, if deemed avoidable.

PURPOSE WITHOUT COMMITMENT

Fifty years into the process aimed at building an ever closer Europe, the EU is a reality throughout Europe and for its twenty-five member states, but it is also a reality for America, whose presence in Europe qualifies it as a virtual member of the Union.

The hard core of that reality is a Euro-Atlantic economy, which no "shock"—real or anticipated—seems able to derail or erode. Transatlantic trade now represents nearly two-fifths of total world trade. Complaints about merchandise trade barriers are surprisingly low—barely 5 percent of total trade during the full decade of the 1990s. The ability to settle "disputes" before they turn into full-fledged trade wars reflects "the mature closeness of an older couple."[38] Trends in foreign direct investment (FDI) are even more relevant because they reveal the unparalleled strength and continued dynamism of the Euro-Atlantic economy since the Cold War. Thus, during the post–Cold War decade of the 1990s, two-way FDI stock grew from a total of $457 billion to $1,550 billion in 2000, with European FDI in the United States growing from roughly $247 billion to almost $900 billion, while U.S. FDI in Europe rose from $215 billion to nearly $650 billion. The numbers are staggering across the board.[39] Cross-border mergers and acquisitions between the United States and Europe grew from $20.6 billion in 1990 to a total of $296 billion in 2000. Since then, these trends have accelerated: despite tensions over Iraq, corporate America invested nearly $87 billion in Europe in 2003, and despite loud antiwar sentiments in Europe, European firms invested nearly $40 billion in America that year. In 2004, the transatlantic economy is that of a virtual state that generates roughly $2.5 trillion in total and largely non-discriminatory commercial sales a year, and employs over 12 million "in-sourced" workers in good, high-wage jobs.

Compared to the proven mutual benefits provided by the Euro-Atlantic economy, accrued from repetitive and continuous investments, American (let alone European) economic relations with Asia have been more speculative and continue to be more risky.[40] They have also resulted in a heavy redistributive cost with unprecedented levels of bilateral trade deficits, and with an expanding deficit in job creation exacerbated by a growing practice of outsourcing jobs to Asia. Moreover, like Europe, many countries in Asia, starting with Japan, suffer from social sclerosis and structural (or, in China, ideological) rigidities that are difficult to overcome. But unlike Europe, Asia lacks a wide multilateral structure for peace, democracy, and prosperity. The countries of Asia cannot rely, therefore, on the kind of institutional order found in the EU, as well as between its members. Unlike Europe, these countries have not yet resolved past territorial and national rivalries, or achieved the balance, and displayed the moderation, which can contain conflicts after they start. And unlike their counterparts in Europe, the governments of Asia have not overcome fundamental social issues—including birth control, environmental issues, or individual and minority rights—that will define their future political stability and economic influence.

That the major wars fought by both superpowers during the second half of the twentieth century took place in Asia is not a coincidence; that outside the Middle East, the major wars fought during the first half of the twenty-first century are likely to take place in Asia should not come as a surprise either. Returning to the image of a maturing or even aged transatlantic couple, the terms of endearment have changed: whatever love may be left between America and Europe, both have accumulated joint assets that make the threat of divorce between them no longer credible. But when it comes to America (let alone Europe) and Asia, the relationship is only beginning: how it develops, and how well, will be neither evident nor convincing for many years to come. No less evident, but equally significant is whether any new relationship with Asia will be pursued by either the United States or the states of Europe at the expense of their partnership.

The distinctive closeness of the Euro-Atlantic couple is not based on shared assets only. It is also based on a shared approach to life and governance at the local, national, and regional levels. During the Cold War, the rise of the EU rekindled that convergence. Charges of a societal drift, which began to escalate in early 2001, fail to show the retroactive perspective needed to measure the transformation of Europe *à l'américaine*. "The American traveler . . . comes to a Europe which is more foreign to Americans today than it has ever been in all our history," wrote Theodore White shortly after World War II.[41] And White added, "This separation of European and American civilizations happens, moreover, at a moment when America is finally more intimately involved in European affairs than ever before in our national history." Since that time, the gap has been bridged sufficiently to leave travelers who now cross the ocean moving from one family residence to another rather than from one civilization to another alien planet. Admittedly, unfolding demographic and cultural changes may loosen this intimacy and create enough "metamorphosis" on each side of the Atlantic, as well as within Europe, to end the synthesis of the past fifty years.[42] Under such circumstances, the partnership would give way to an estrangement that would, at best, mean a multispeed Euro-Atlantic community in which the United States would relate most closely to a few European states (for the most part not in the euro-zone) that did not follow the pace of a European Union and would now want to limit to an expanded free-trade area. But that is hardly a reality yet, and pending more evidence to the contrary, the common home that has emerged over the past several decades is still standing.

Still, this is a strange home that defies precedents, logic, and definition as it responds to a delicate and "unprecedented balance among supranational, subnational, and national governments."[43] Lacking a clear and undisputed center of decision—a president, a parliament, an army— Europe remains voiceless; when it is heard, the cacophonic tones that come through are those of "a federal non-state" that hopes to achieve "what Hamilton would have regarded as either disastrous or impossible—the separation of law from the power to enforce it."[44] Indeed, little seems to have changed since Constantinople fell to the Turks in 1454: "There is no reverence and no obedience; we look on pope and emperor as figureheads and empty titles. Every city state has its king and there are as many princes as there are households."[45] Over time, no attempt to achieve unity by force ever succeeded, or at least no longer than the time needed for a coalition—a counterweight—to defeat it.[46] As a result, hegemonies in Europe rose and fell, exhausted by their bids for dominance— depopulated Spain, tiny Holland, disintegrating Austria, wary France, and defeated Germany—and unable to match the power available at the periphery of Europe and beyond—Britain, of course, but also Russia and, ultimately, America.

What also made each bid for dominance a precursor of the bid that followed was that every peripheral state used to restore Europe's precarious balance next attempted to impose its will on the continent after victory had been achieved. For over 300 years, that often was the case for a Russian state that expanded steadily westward without ever joining the European state system—reportedly one Belgium a year, on the average.[47] The Russian bid was extended one last time after 1945, and it was contained one more time by the Anglo-Saxon island powers of the West who had little taste for territorial gains after each of the European wars they waged and usually won. For nineteenth-century Britain, there were other imperial opportunities that were less risky, a world away, than a territorial grab across the English Channel. For twentieth-century America, Europe was the continent in opposition to which America was born, and that remained true even after staying home away from the Old World ceased to be possible, however desirable that choice might have been otherwise.

Protected from Russia by the United States, and with little to fear from another burst of imperial energy from postwar Britain, continental Europe could embark upon its new project at a moment of unprecedented balance and homogeneity in Western Europe. Little remained of Germany, and even less was thought of entrusting Germany with a European leadership to which it could no longer aspire. This, after all, was the country that had brought the United States back to Europe twice, and these were the people against whom Europe's grand coalitions had been formed twice in slightly more than a generation. In any case, after 1945 only half of Germany was left—with the other half grabbed by the Soviet Union, and even that Western half, the Federal Republic, was busy reinventing itself as a democratic and pacifist state. As to France, it might still have the required attitude for empire but it no longer had the capabilities needed to keep it or the will expected to fight for it. Indeed, France's final bid for hegemony in Europe ended during Napoleon's painful retreat from Russia in 1812: after that, France never won another significant European war alone. Nor could France still play multipolar games of balance with a renewed bid for postwar security with Russia: in December 1944, de Gaulle's alliance with Moscow was a wartime union of convenience sought in anticipation of a temporary postwar political alignment in France where, de Gaulle knew as well as his counterpart in Italy, room would have to be made for the Communist Party to enter the coalition majorities needed to govern either country.

With no state in Western Europe able to assert alone its leadership of Europe, the postwar history of European unity has been shaped by the evolution of bilateral relations between France, Great Britain, and Germany. Like the history of Europe's relations with the United States, this history is replete with headlines of shared tensions and rivalries—France and Britain against or without Germany, and France and Germany without or in spite of Britain. After 1945, Britain was France's partner of choice, and the initial Anglo-French *pas de deux* was staged from the 1947 Dunkirk Treaty to the aborted bilateral deal of Rambouillet, in December 1962, between de Gaulle and Harold Macmillan. The Anglo-Saxon choreography arranged for a French musical score was wrong, however. The one *pirouette* that had made prewar Britain great—keep Europe at a distance while conquering a distant empire—demanded qualities that kept postwar Britain small, now that it no longer enjoyed its imperial holdings, while its governments dismissed the potential of the European idea. Britain lived to regret that choice: the process launched in the 1950s was ripe for its leadership as an alternative to France's or as a counterweight to Germany's. That London chose to ignore its French partner's repeated pleas—to build a European Steel and Coal Community, to start a European Defense Community, and to join a European Economic Community—hurt Britain even more than Europe. In late 2000, how ironic it was to hear Blair tell his listeners in Poland of Britain's mistaken decisions to "stand apart . . . marginalized and isolated" from Europe as a "benign, avuncular friend" periodically faced with "the choice [of] catching up or staying out."[48]

After London said no, seemingly one last time in early 1963, France's bid for the leadership of Europe focused on Germany, from the Franco-German Treaty of Friendship in January 1963 until the political defeat of Chancellor Helmut Kohl in September 1998. That, however, demanded a degree of confidence that had been missing at least since Germany's unification. The factors that restored confidence in France were not French made. Rather they included the reality of Germany's military occupation, including U.S. occupation, as well as the certainty of Germany's division following its postwar territorial amputation farther in the East, both guaranteed by the Soviet army. Should an occupied, divided, and amputated Germany not be enough to assuage French anxieties, the Fifth Republic could also rely, entering the 1960s, on achievements of its own: an ascending economy, a stabilized polity that ended the "wars of the Republics" waged since the 1789 Revolution, and a controlling *force de frappe* that ended Germany's intrinsic superiority. Still, trust came slowly. Responding to a dutifully impressed Henry Kissinger who had asked him, in early 1969, "how [he] will keep Germany from dominating the Europe [he] had just described," de Gaulle, "seized by profound melancholy at so much obtuseness," responded—"*par la guerre*" ("through war").[49]

For thirty-odd years, the process of European integration evolved mainly around France and Germany because neither viewed Britain as a valid alternative. In Paris and in Bonn, Britain's hostility to Europe, even after it joined the Community in 1973, stood in the way of a close relationship. As Tony Blair put it in late 2001, "The tragedy for . . . Britain has been that politicians of both parties have consistently failed to appreciate the emerging reality of European integration. And in doing so, they have failed Britain's interests . . . in the name of illusions."[50] In addition, Paris feared London's ties with the United States, as well as its related predilection for NATO over Europe, while Bonn resented London's apparent indifference to its security concerns and its preference for negotiations over containment. Even though the end of the Cold War brought Mitterrand momentarily closer to Margaret Thatcher (who shared the French president's anxieties about Germany's reunification), close relations with Germany remained at the center of the French ambitious EU agenda adopted in Maastricht in December 1991, and enforced in subsequent years under the co-leadership of Mitterrand and Helmut Kohl. In 1998, the rise of Gerhard Schroeder seemed to open the door for closer bilateral relations between Germany and Britain, at a time when Blair was also seeking closer bilateral relations with France. Neither worked, and Franco-German relations remained at the center of a "euro-ic" agenda that Blair could endorse only partially while waiting for Britain to adopt the euro—until that, too, was derailed, first by the war in Iraq and the extraordinary personal tensions that built up between Blair and Jacques Chirac, and next by the unexpected call for a national referendum over the constitutional treaty and the dramatic consequences that a rejection of the treaty might have for both Britain and the EU.

Over the years, the United States has added complexity to intra-European relations by maintaining, or even initiating, special relationships with Britain and Germany to counter French relations with either country, and also to boost U.S. influence in Europe. In January 1963, de Gaulle's objections to Britain's entry in the Common Market were said to reflect his view of Britain as a Trojan horse for the United States. But it is now a full stable of Trojan horses that a larger EU must accommodate since its enlargement to the East in May 2004. A larger Europe with a different center of gravity means that two countries only are no longer sufficient to manage the process of integration within the EU and relative to the United States—whether France and either Germany or Britain in the Union, or America with either Britain or Germany in the Alliance, or even America, Britain, France, and Germany as a so-called quad within NATO. That should reassure European skeptics who still fear a malign American hand that guides the EU at the expense of European interests, as well as American skeptics who resent the malevolent French hand that promotes Europe at the expense of U.S. interests. In sum, there cannot be more Europe without Britain, and there need not be less of America to have more Europe.

The new choreography needed for Europe's "final" curtain call demands more, not fewer, states committed to lead the Union—at three (with Britain), or at five (with Italy and Spain), or at more (with Poland and others). But the need for more integration also extends to relations between the EU and the United States, a virtual nonmember member state of the Union, as well as EU relations with NATO, where the EU is already found as an invisible member of an organization whose new global mandate, first asserted at the NATO Prague Summit in November 2002, calls for nonmilitary assets that the EU is more qualified to provide than its institutional transatlantic counterpart. As Samuel Huntington has stated, "the idea of integration" is "the successor idea to containment."[51] More specifically, integration is about locking a group of countries into policies that address common concerns and produce mutually shared benefits, "and then building institutions that lock them in even more." This latter imperative, adds Amitai Etzioni, is all the more compelling as the "halfway integration" that now characterizes both the European Union and the Atlantic Community to which it is linked "cannot be sustained" and must either move to a higher level of integration, including supranationality, or "fall back to a lower one."[52]

Admittedly, a call for more integration (leaving aside the perennial debate over supranationality) will be heard with some anxiety in Europe and some wariness in the United States: the purpose is understood, but the commitment is resisted. But if not in the EU, where; if not with the United States, with whom; if not now, when and, perhaps above all, what else instead? Better to set America's alarm clock at half before the EU—

early enough, that is, for the United States to wake up to the institutional reality it helped launch after World War II, unfinished but usable, and separated from the United States but no longer separable. Better also to set Europe's watch at half past NATO—early enough, that is, for the countries of Europe to prepare for the contributions they must make within NATO if they are to achieve at last their escape from subjugation without facing the risks of isolation. Some will say—What's the rush? But as learned many times over the past two decades—most recently on September 11, 2001—even the long term is finite. As sudden and unpredictable events force history to leap forward and in unexpected directions, opportunities that are spurned in the short term may never reappear. America and Europe have ample and good reasons to be exasperated with, and even fearful of, their difficult partnership. But neither wants or can afford a separation, let alone a divorce, because both know that life without the other would be less affluent, less safe, and ultimately less satisfying.

5

POWER AND ORDER

The infamous events of September 11, 2001, changed America's vision of the world and the dangers it raises for the nation's security and its citizens' safety. Trying to understand these events with theoretical abstractions is to risk another failure in a place and at a time that no one can predict notwithstanding the predictable enormity of its consequences.[1] As a result, the events of September 11 are also transforming the U.S. role in the world and, therefore, its relations with other countries. When addressing the wars of 911—no longer understood as a single day but rather as a year because of the medieval nature of those wars—America's vision has become less convincing, its role less benign, and its policies less flexible. The struggle for the soul of American foreign policy is no longer over a choice between power and principles, with the latter standing in the way of defining the order that could be enforced by the former. Rather, the struggle is between the politics of power and the politics of force, with the latter used to prevent, preempt, and eliminate threats, rather than neglect, contain, and belatedly defeat them.[2] Even more narrowly, the struggle is no longer over whether and even why to use force (and with whom), but where and when (and against whom).

As was the case in 1948, the foreign policy and security debate that erupted during the 2004 presidential campaign was not over whether to wage the global war on terror unveiled during the previous three years. "My opponent says he has a plan," argued President Bush during his second debate with Senator John F. Kerry, on October 8, 2004. "Sounds familiar because it is called the Bush plan." Each plan echoed the other, and Kerry also echoed the president when he pledged to "not stop in our effort to hunt down and kill terrorists" and "never give a veto over American security to any other entity—not a nation, not a country, not an institution." The question was not over what had been done on the basis of what was thought to be known at the time but why and how well it had been done in the context of what should have been planned prior to the action; nor were questions raised over the wars that had been started in Afghanistan and Iraq, but when and how those wars could be ended there and elsewhere.

This debate goes beyond Bush and beyond Iraq. Over the next decade or two, no U.S. president will be able to deny a readiness to use force if, where, and when it is deemed necessary, notwithstanding the risks of miscalculation which will be repeatedly faced when confronting adversaries that fail for the most part to meet Western standards of rationality and outright humanity. It is sad that in the face of the barbaric attacks endured thus far and likely to be repeated in the future, "a pagan ethos" is taking hold in the United States, even if it must be occasionally enforced at the expense of the principles America has cherished historically.[3] Nor will any U.S. president in the next decade or two be able to call for a significant reduction in defense spending: In the post-9/11 world, a strategy of preponderance is designed to serve the nation and its citizens on whose behalf the nation's superior capabilities must be maintained and used.[4] But because the new American zeal for military action is not shared in Europe and in other parts of the world, the U.S. preponderance is also emerging as a serious cause for global concern, and a cause for widening public resentment abroad. For away from America, and most of all across the Atlantic, there is a predilection for the nonmilitary dimensions of power and added emphasis on the deeper requirements of justice. In sum, the choice is not between power and weakness in a Hobbesian world where the latter is at the mercy of the former, but between power and order in a neoliberal world where institutions regulate over the strong and the weak alike.

Because neither of these two visions is entirely right, neither is entirely wrong either. That the American view of the world changed in the fall of 2001 is not merely a matter of perceptions. The world did change, and interstate relations, too, were changed by these events. As Jean-Paul Sartre urged forty years ago, "come close and listen [to] strangers gathered around a fire; for they are talking of the destiny they will mete out to your trading centers and to the hired soldiers who defend them."[5] This "suppressed fury" and "irrepressible violence," he added, "at times reviving old and terrible myths, at others binding themselves by scrupulous rites," would not be "the resurrection of savage instincts, nor even the effect of resentment: it is man recreating itself."

These words sound more credible now than when Sartre wrote them, as an introduction to Fritz Fanon's passionate plea on behalf of the "Wretched of the Earth" who populated the European empires at the time—and whose rebellion against their condition was anticipated as the dominant theme of their time. In a narrow sense, September 11 confirmed the will of some radical extremists to hijack and mobilize a religion against the "distant enemy"—a cultural coalition of U.S.-led Western countries that protects the "near enemy" at home, whether in Saudi Arabia, Pakistan, or elsewhere. The ultimate goal of the "war" imagined by Osama bin Laden and his followers—"until Islamic rule is here on earth"—is to restore the purity of the Islamic man, a purity that allegedly ceased to exist in the thirteenth century when the rule of the Islamic clerics ended. Only a militant interpretation of the Koran can prevent the further spread of the pervasive Western ideas that have infiltrated Islam: it cannot be allowed to succeed.[6] In an even broader sense, these events point to the nihilistic anger that has been building up in vast areas of the world where the state does not exist, or, when it does exist, fails to respond to its citizens' minimal expectations, material as well as spiritual. Saddam Hussein's Iraq was neither a follower of bin Laden's quest for purity or a proponent of such nihilistic anger. He was not specifically linked to the attacks of September 11. But the more Saddam found it expedient to associate his regime to bin Laden's words and deeds, the more he became a risk that, after September 11, 2001, could no longer be dismissed or even ignored. In the prevailing mindset, the issue was not even over whether there was undeniable evidence that he was an imminent threat, but whether he might be, now or ever. That alone was a risk not worth taking, and even the subsequent discovery that he had no weapons of mass destruction was not sufficient to reappraise the decision to remove him by force.

There is more to the war on terror, however. After three global wars and a near infinite number of regional and civil conflicts, the twentieth century has added to an already long list of winners and losers.[7] Now there is a new generation of "wretched" people who live in, or attempt to escape, the territorial corpses left behind by these wars—wars of territorial expansion, wars of national liberation, and even wars of spiritual redemption. In most cases, these are not wars that America started, and in many cases, these were wars that America did not even fight; but these are wars to which America can no longer remain indifferent. In 2003, Iraq, coming a few months after Afghanistan, was the central theater for one such war—unlikely to be the last, alas, as if August 1914 had been initially limited to a bilateral military confrontation in Serbia, between, say, Austria-Hungary and Russia, and over unresolved territorial or dynastic issues inherited from the collapse of the Ottoman Empire and the unraveling of the Habsburg Empire. Looming ahead, there would still have been the larger war that, we now know all too well, involved much more than Serbia because it dealt with the inability to organize a new security order in Europe after Germany's unification and on the eve of the Soviet revolution. In 2003, like in 1914, going to war might be explained and even justified on the basis of what was known at the time; what is more difficult to explain or justify is how the postwar years were managed in the context of what was known before the start of the war. To this day in the case of World War I, that was and is likely to remain inexcusable. With regard to the war in Iraq, our concerns and even indignation over the initial mistakes are still incomplete pending the ability of future historians to consider what was done in and beyond 2005 before they can render their final verdict.

Even more than other countries whose history has been more tragic and less rewarding, the United States is ill at ease in a world in which a permanent threat of terror calls for an unprecedented reliance on military force. People whose desperation makes them seek death as relief from life are relying on levels of violence that invite more violence. When the use of absolute means takes precedence over the quest for plausible ends, perpetrators and victims stand as judge-penitents, as Albert Camus put it. Sentences inflicted on the perpetrators are to be endured as well when victims, tormented by what was done to them, become possessed by the need for justice. Even as we question the reasons that brought our adversaries to such a condition, the violence they use defines a twisted morality that threatens to engulf us as well—kill in order to not be killed and, therefore, better wrong than unsafe. "I begin by proposing unlimited freedom, but end in absolute despotism," confessed Shigalyov, the theoretician of the nihilists in Dostoievsky's *The Possessed*.[8] This is the sad truth that permeates the emerging global anarchy.

Traditional rules of war and peace no longer apply when internal conflicts and international wars are waged on the same battleground. Left alone, so-called failed states fall into the pattern of "praetorian politics" described by Samuel Huntington at the peak of the Cold War. "The wealthy bribe; students riot; workers strike; mobs demonstrate; and the military coup."[9] That is no longer all, however. There is worse: for now, as the zealots preach, the followers kill, at home (or at least where they happen to reside or congregate) but also abroad wherever the innocents might live and congregate. The terror thus caused is an affront to justice. But because the retaliation that follows may also be devoid of justice, the just and the criminal coexist in ways that are understandable at home, but not in other parts of the world where there is less of a will to separate them.

The paradox, then, is that winning the war somewhere may require actions that will prolong it elsewhere, whether at a place and time of "our" own choosing or at a place and time chosen by others. "Only the complete destruction of international terrorism and the regimes that sponsor it will spare America from further attack," warned Senator John McCain shortly after September 11.[10] That early warning, repeated by many since, is not a small ambition. But what will be left to rebuild after everything has been destroyed, including a cultural "mindset" that embodies more than we can understand and is forced to absorb more than we can forget? The mythical "days after" the war—when winners attend to the losers for absolution of their respective sins—threaten to last long past Bush and the war he chose to wage in Iraq, just as the previous global war, the Cold War, went on long past Truman and the war he chose to wage in Korea. Memories of postwar Germany and Japan are meant to reassure on the basis of assumptions that seem naïve when describing the scope and nature of the conflicts ahead. Since May 1, 2003, the debate between America and the world has not been about the benefits of liberation for the Iraqi people and their neighbors, but about all that was needed to achieve that lofty goal after the war had been won—occupation, pacification, reconstruction, and rehabilitation. In the absence of more effective plans for postwar Iraq, the analogy more likely to return might be that of *revanchistes* enemies in 1919 rather than that of defeated regimes in 1945.

"No course open to the United States is free of risk," noted Deputy Secretary of Defense Paul Wolfowitz three months before the war in Iraq.[11] "The value of this victory is incalculable," he added shortly after the war—"nothing less than our security and the peace of the world." Neither then nor since was Wolfowitz the only eminent American to hold this view. Nor was this view exclusive to America. In the early spring of 2003, many in Europe and elsewhere readily agreed that Iraq—the region and the world—without Saddam would be safer. But not safe: whatever the merits of the new U.S.-made scale of acceptable risks when "weighing the risks of action against the risks of inaction," it invites legitimate concern elsewhere as the guns of August 1914 are heard again—arguably even before they are fired. Where is the next stop along the way to ending the "axis of evil"—and who decides? In 2004, the emphasis was no longer placed on the "incalculable" gains that would result from victory but on the "unthinkable" consequences of failure.[12] In 2005, emphasis might return to the "unthinkable" consequences of inaction in the face of its "incalculable" risks raised by its "evil" regime in some other place like Iran.

IMPERIAL AMERICA

The peerless nature of American power does not foreclose the need for like-minded and capable allies. This is not just a matter of choice. A principal weakness of an imperial power is that however overwhelming its preponderance may be, power never stays in one place, and irresistibly moves on to other ascending states or coalitions of lesser states. Thus, no imperial order can or does last. Already, most nations are ambivalent about the desirability of the current unipolar moment, which suggests ambivalence over what America is—the sole superpower. But they also seem seriously concerned about the aftermath of that moment, which means a concern over what America does, and how well—no longer with and for others, but on its own and to others. In short, there is concern in the world for what America is, as well as for what it does: at the peak of its power, America's ability to sustain its leadership has eroded because its leaders' credibility has fallen to its lowest point.

Beyond anything that relates specifically to President Bush and his administration, this is what the debate over the use of American power in Iraq was all about: a test of the world's capacity to challenge the seemingly unlimited U.S. ability to use force with a zeal that made people around the world all the more suspicious and fearful as the explanations provided for the decision to go to war proved to be wrong while the expectations that surrounded the hopes to end it proved to be fatally flawed.

To Americans of all political veins, this condition is cause for dismay, exasperation, and even anger. As a fact of birth, America was not born into the world to become a power in the world like Europe, but to escape its debilitating ways away from Europe—to build in a New World the dream that the first waves of European immigrants could not happily live in their native habitat. As a matter of conviction, America's rise as a world power was not meant as a substitute for falling or defunct empires, but as a tool to end the age of empires—to assert the inalienable right of self-determination and the primacy of justice for all over the arbitrary control of distant and exploitative imperial powers. Admittedly, the Cold War modified the conditions of America's birth. The United States returned to the Old World where its presence now exceeds that of most EU members—not as a European power but at the very least as a power in Europe. That, however, was a consensual decision—meaning a decision that was made by Europeans who wanted to rely on the United States for the security they needed, and by Americans who needed to rely on Europe to build the order they wanted.

Admittedly, the events of September 11 may well have derailed that consensus, including America's anti-imperial convictions and notwithstanding repeated claims to the contrary.[13] Yet, whatever temptation there may be for the United States to use the current imperial moment to maximize its gains, with others if it can and unilaterally if it must, the greatest obstacle to an American Empire is not the counterweight provided by a single country or group of countries in and beyond Europe. The greatest obstacle is America itself, a nation that abhors the imperial methods—kill and be killed—and does not enjoy its benefits—least of all territorial conquests or even control. This is a "post-heroic" imperial power that still wishes to be "debellicized" but nonetheless does what it must in the absence of readily available alternatives.[14]

Nation or empire? The question is not new, and there have been other moments of U.S. preponderance when it was raised with comparable anxiety and even urgency. Indeed, much of the Cold War was lived under conditions of flawed bipolarity. In the East, the Soviet Union remained an incomplete power because of a glaring lack of economic capabilities, because its interests remained mostly regional notwithstanding the Kremlin's aborted rise to globalism later on, and because its saliency was explicitly limited by the resistance its ideology met whenever it was not imposed by Soviet force. In the West, U.S. defense spending nearly trebled that of all other NATO allies by 1960—and overwhelmed Soviet capabilities notwithstanding mythical notions of a "missile gap" between the two superpowers.[15] On occasion, these early moments of U.S. preponderance also produced the fact or the appearance of self-defeating arrogance. In the 1960s, a bubble of interventionist exuberance burst in Southeast Asia that unveiled the illusions that had caused it: illusion of a superior efficacy that guaranteed America's victories, and illusion of a superior hubris that asserted their legitimacy. But these moments of U.S. preponderance and arrogance were short lived as Americans themselves remained skeptical of the threat identified by their leaders and rebelled against an interventionist zeal that tore the fabric of the nation and even, for a brief moment, threatened to disassemble it.

Preponderance is not the issue, however. What is an issue is the use of that preponderance in ways that invite failure, for lack of judgment, lack of will, or lack of competence. For then, shrewdly observed political scientist Christopher Layne many years before September 2001, "instead of letting History take its time to allow countervailing forces to emerge, unfinished states launch their challenge to unwilling states."[16] Past the Cold War and entering a new century, America's reputation in the world was such that its power could have been welcomed as the most effective protection for the nation and its allies, as well as the most endearing agent for change in states that the democratic revolutions started by the United States during the Cold War had not reached yet. That was the real unipolar moment, one during which a strategy of preponderance might have been a winning strategy, once more extended at the invitation of America's like-minded friends, and readily endorsed by states who had missed out on the advantages of intimacy with the preponderant power. For that power—"America's hegemony"—had a benign reputation and a universal reach that made it, in the words of the then-EU External Relations Commissioner Chris Patten, "no bad thing if others must adapt themselves to U.S. preferences."[17] Indeed, what is most surprising about the prewar debate over Iraq is how quickly the Bush administration lost the overwhelming influence it had at the UN Security Council: less than four months after it had gained unanimous support for its views in early November 2002, eleven of its remaining fourteen members, including Chile and Mexico, opposed a U.S.-sponsored resolution for its immediate enforcement.

To argue, as it is done, that containment is not relevant to the post-9/11 threats seems reasonable for anyone who lived that day in the United States, and feared its recurrence afterward. "As a matter of common sense and self defense," argued Bush in September 2002, "shadowy networks of individuals" and "falling" or "rogue" states intent on perpetrating "premeditated, politically motivated violence . . . against innocents" cannot be allowed "to strike first"—especially with "weapons of mass destruction as weapons of choice." The logic is indisputable because the danger is real. What changed most dramatically on September 11, 2001, was, therefore, the arithmetic of risk taking. Even if it were to be granted that realities on the ground had remained the same—the same lack of clarity about what Saddam Hussein or others were doing or could do, and the same uncertainties about capabilities available to Saddam Hussein and others like him—the assessment of these realities had been profoundly modified. "Events," wrote the historian A. J. P. Taylor in a wonderful portrait of Bismarck, "were stronger than the plans of men."[18] As a result, what was also changed on September 11 was the willingness to accept any of the presumptions loosely made about Saddam's capabilities and prudence because of a new awareness of what the consequences of a mistake might be—consequences that could no longer be either ignored or dismissed. Late in 2002, a 60 percent probability (or 40 or 80 percent) that no threat from Iraq justified an immediate use of force against its regime became a 100 percent certainty that force must be used because, however wrong it might be to wage the war early, it would be unsafe and potentially irresponsible to not wage it or even wage it later.

This logic may be valid in the short term, but what follows from it can have long-term consequences that will lack logic for the world order to which America and its allies aspire. An occasional and extraordinary need for unilateral and even preemptive action because of a danger that is not clear to all, and is convincingly imminent only to a few, cannot be worked into a "doctrine" applicable for the establishment of an international order aimed at a wide variety of elusive and distant risks. Over the years, America's uniqueness as a nation among other nations has not been its lust for power but its passion for order, an order that would be not only stable but also an order that would be just. Nothing would be so disturbing, indeed repugnant, as to see the United States share the imperial fate of the great powers in opposition to which it was born but which it would now pursue through a misplaced sense of obligation.[19]

Adopted by the United States, but soon of increasing appeal to others as well, a strategy of preemptive action would become a sure recipe for a new international disorder based on the ability of the strong to inflict pain on its weaker neighbor, unless the distant superpower stands itself in the way with preventive or retaliatory threats of its own. This is brinksmanship that belongs to another age, fifty years ago, when then-Secretary of State John Foster Dulles urged America "to take chances" in order to demonstrate its will to "go to the brink" because otherwise all would be "lost."[20] It echoes, too, the same "crusading spirit" preached by the administration that shaped the Cold War after Truman had acknowledged it—the crusading spirit of the early American republic when, added

Dulles, "we were darn sure that what we had was a lot better than what anybody else had."[21] That spirit faded in Vietnam, but it is the same spirit—the "illusion of omnipotence," as it was called during the Korean War—that has motivated the Bush administration and much of the nation since September 11. Heard for what it is, President Bush's view of America as the sole existing "national model for national success," his pride in the nation's "unparalleled military strength and great economic and political influence," and his unusually stubborn denial of any mistake of execution if not of intent are imperial attributes par excellence. However factually justified these attributes may be, they often condemn the imperial power to doing much more than it can, and to completing much less than it must. In due time, the discovery of these limits has always come with considerable pain for all, the imperial-ist but also the imperial-ized that do not want to stay at the mercy of the imperial power's benign and peaceful intentions.

These concerns transcend Bush and the events of September 11 because they resurrect an unsettled debate over the limits of American power and the U.S. will to use that power relative to what the nation is and thinks of itself. As has been shown often in the past, a rhetoric used at home to justify policy can become policy abroad if it is repeated often enough—if, that is, Americans and others around the world, friends and foes alike, come to expect that the United States will do as it says, even if its leaders do not always say what they do.[22] Admittedly, the sense of danger that is felt in the United States now is different from the threats that conditioned earlier Cold War decisions to commit American power, and eventually use it with increasing frequency until the pattern was broken in Vietnam. "The most affirmative truth we hold," said then-Secretary of State Dean Acheson in January 1950 "is the dignity and right of every individual to develop in their own way, making their own mistakes, reaching their own triumphs but acting under their own responsibility."[23] Such a "truth" is compelling so long as "we" do not suffer the consequences of "their" mistakes. Thus, the novelty of the present environment is over the indivisibility of a global order from which even the United States, an invulnerable nation for most of its history, cannot escape.

With distance no longer a guarantee for the citizens' safety and the nation's security, the risks of overextension are more real than during the Cold War. A comparison between Vietnam, the classic case of U.S. military intervention during the Cold War, and Iraq, the most notable case since September 11 and the Cold War, helps to make the point. In the end, failure in Vietnam was of no lasting geopolitical consequence for the Cold War—within a few years, America was back, the alliance was renewed, and the Soviet Union was gone. In 2004, no one dared make such projections about Iraq where the consequences of failure would be serious and lasting for all.

More broadly, and past Iraq, the potential for U.S. overextension in the post-9/11 world was previewed by the Bush administration in August 2003, with a dramatic call for a "generational commitment" to the transformation of the Greater Middle East, a vast region extending from North Africa to the Persian Gulf and encompassing twenty-two countries, none of them truly democratic and many of them hostile, with a combined population of over 300 million people, most of them very young, very poor, and very angry—especially at the United States. To make its vision readily understandable, the example of postwar Europe was used as an "important historical analogy" that would not only explain how an entire region could be saved from itself but also, and perhaps above all, as a reassuring precedent that confirmed that it could be done.[24]

The example is admittedly important, and the analogy may even be irresistible, but it is a historical distortion that is dangerously misleading: if Bush is to resemble Truman during moments that are equally decisive, then he and his advisers ought to have a better sense of the conditions that shaped Truman's decisions and determined their successful outcome. To be sure, as we have seen, U.S. policies helped Europe discover the innumerable benefits of democracy, reconciliation, and peace after decades of brutal and inhuman conflicts, but the Europeans did not have to be taught the benefits of democracy and human rights, as compared to a region in which there has never been a democratic revolution. Even more importantly, in Europe, unlike anywhere else, the United States was "the missing component in a situation which might otherwise be solved," as Dean Acheson had put it shortly after World War II. Why that was the case had to do with the facts of Europe's conditions at the time. In 1945, none of the European countries that were to join the United States in an Atlantic Alliance, and none of the fewer countries that were to start a European community, considered itself a "winner" of the war that had just ended—with the exception of Britain, which had entered the conflict from the beginning and fought it till it was won (and, pointedly enough, subsequently chose to stay out of a European Community that Britain dismissed as a community of losers). Among former European Great Powers that might wish to pretend otherwise, including France, none still viewed another war in Europe as desirable to achieve any reasonable national objective. There was, in short, a will for peace that was credible because the will for war had been exhausted.

Moreover, after 1945 the chosen few that were to transform Europe displayed unusual homogeneity: a political setting with mostly Christian-Democratic coalition governments at the helm; attachment to parliamentarian traditions; territorial contiguity, with parity of resources in size and population (especially after the division of Germany made it the equal of the other "large" European countries, including France, Italy, and Belgium, Luxembourg, and the Netherlands combined); comparable needs for postwar reconstruction and a similar public urge for lasting reconciliation; and no more irreconcilable territorial claims after the cases of Trieste and the Saar had been peacefully settled less than ten years after the war had ended. The sense of powerlessness that prevailed in the region, as well as a widespread will for self-abdication, had them "invite" the United States to help—to act as a catalyst for the transformation that followed. Europe's receptiveness to the terms set—indeed, imposed—by the United States, and America's responsiveness to Europe's invitation, also had to do with an American political culture that on the whole Europeans recognized and with which they could identify.

It should be obvious that none of these conditions are met in the Middle East, however defined. Nor is it "condescending" to argue, as Condoleezza Rice claimed during her early presentations of the new American vision, that these conditions are unlikely to be met any time soon. Warning against "the belief that it is possible to democratize governments, anytime, anywhere, under any circumstances," Jeane Kirkpatrick, an early guru of neo-conservative thinking, warned that "decades, if not centuries, are normally required for people to acquire the necessary disciplines and habits" of democracy.[25] Extending that warning to the Middle East, especially if enlarged to Pakistan and Afghanistan, is not to suggest that people who live there are not ready for self-government, or that their past does not qualify them for the democratic future envisioned for them—even though that evocation, too, requires an extraordinary leap of faith and a better informed understanding of the principles that would shape the adoption of democratic institutions in an Islamic country. But unlike post-1945 Europe, the Middle East remains populated by many states, groups within those states, and people throughout and beyond the region who believe in war—wars that must still be waged because they can still be won—and for whom, therefore, the use of organized force and indiscriminate violence remain reliable tools to settle the distribution of land, the allocation of resources, and the legitimacy of authority throughout the region. In other words, if linking Europe and the Middle East provides for "an important analogy," it would be more apt to evoke conditions in Europe after World War I rather than after World War II—which means that the "generational commitment" which the Bush administration began to envision in August 2003 will include a great deal of disorder and conflicts before peace can be imposed, as it was on Germany, and a new regional order born, let alone built, as it was in Europe.

Nor is an analogy between post-1945 Germany and post-2003 Iraq any better.[26] In fact, it is much worse and, mercifully, faded from the official discourse in 2004 when a need for stability seemed to take precedence over the more distant goal of democracy. The best that can be said about post-Saddam Iraq is that it lacks the three vital dimensions of Germany's recovery after 1945. First, there was a German will to reinvent itself—to become something else, as if Germany had never existed before. "When you fall from the heights as we Germans have done," Theodor Heuss noted, "you realize that it is necessary to break with what has been."[27] To break with its past, its political institutions and traditions, there was also a homogeneous German people who proved to be as equally committed to being "good" as they had been united in being evil during the previous decade. The rehabilitation of the German state—through denazification, disarmament, democratization, and even territorial (and constitutional) dismemberment—was quickly achieved because the qualities that had made it possible for the Germans to build a war machine that fought a worldwide coalition to a draw for more than two years could be recycled to build a model of economic efficiency, political stability, and national self-abdication. Finally, to lead a hybrid nation into the future, there was the homemade leadership provided by the first German chancellor, Konrad Adenauer, who could also rely on the unusual discipline of his political opposition to build a lasting consensus on behalf of his policies. It should have been apparent to all that such conditions did not exist, and could not be readily created, in Iraq—because of its character, its people, its history, or its leadership after the hateful regime had been changed. That it was not immediately so apparent to the postwar planners of the Bush administration is cause for wonder and worse.

Making of Iraq the model for democratizing the Muslim world was a creative fantasy, not only because of the predictable difficulties that would be met when enforcing that goal in Iraq proper but also because of the predictable instabilities that would accompany similar efforts among Iraq's neighbors. It may well be that the goal echoed the Reagan doctrine whose enforcement at the expense of President Ferdinand Marcos in the Philippines set the stage for the democratic revolutions that ended the Cold War during the latter half of the 1980s—in South Korea, Taiwan, and Tiananmen Square, but also in Latin America, starting with Nicaragua and El Salvador, and, most of all, in Eastern Europe and ultimately the Soviet Union. "The best antidote to communism is democracy," wrote Paul Wolfowitz as Marcos, a long-standing U.S. protégé, was living his last days in office.[28] After the Cold War, the focus changed but the logic remains the same: democracy remains as the best antidote to the spread of terror. But assimilating the democratic transformation of Iraq and the Middle East to the transformation of postwar Germany and Europe recalls the conditions that prevailed after 1919 rather than those that emerged in 1945—and, by implication, creates a disturbing parallel between the use of U.S. force against Iraq in 2003 with the use of French force against Germany in 1923. The most that could be said of Iraq at the close of "major combat operations" in May 2003 is that like old Germany, Iraq lived in a dangerous region, but unlike Germany there was little evidence of its centrality to the stability of an area primarily defined by an Arab-Israeli conflict to which Iraq was relatively marginal over the years.

After 1919, and worse yet after 1923, prospects for a Western coalition collapsed because of an inability to agree on a common strategy toward the Franco-German conflict, the center of future instabilities in Europe; after 2004, prospects for an enlargement of the coalition of the willing would also begin with a sustainable agreement for a common strategy toward the Israeli-Palestinian conflict, which remains at the center of future instabilities in the Middle East.

The point is that false analogies will not help the United States face up to "the security challenge and the moral mission of our time." As was shown during the unexpectedly difficult occupation of Iraq that followed the fall and the capture of Saddam Hussein, people in the region are no more eager to have the United States define the terms of an alleged "third way"—neither the status quo of corrupt oligarchies nor the degrading alternative of Islamic fundamentalism—than Americans appear eager to make the multigenerational commitment of blood and treasures needed to attend to this mission—unless, as was done by President Truman after 1945, they can be convinced that such a mission is imperative and that it will not have to be pursued alone. Nor, for that matter, is it self-evident that a reformed, stabilized, and affluent Middle East would ignore nationalist and religious impulses that are fundamentally contrary to U.S. interests—the same impulses that are currently fought on behalf of these interests. "Man is not born to solve the problems of the world," Goethe once wrote, "but to search for the starting point of the problem and then remain within the limits of what he can comprehend."[29] That is good advice—not only what can be comprehended but also what can be accomplished. Forsaking the status quo in pursuit of democratic ideals is commendable and it may even be imperative in the Middle East. But who will restore the status quo if these democratic ideals prove to be beyond reach?

"U.S. preponderance," wrote Zbigniew Brzezinski at the close of the Cold War, "is both a reality and an illusion."[30] The reality has to do with the facts of American global power, but the illusion has to do with the global authority that such power permits. The transformation of the Middle East is a legitimate goal, but it is a goal that falls outside the range of America's authority to command, and beyond the reach of American preponderance to achieve alone. However necessary America's leadership will be in seeking the fulfillment of this goal, it will not be sufficient. Failure to comprehend these limits would dangerously threaten to set the stage for the failures of post–Cold War, post-9/11 U.S. policies not only there but also in Europe and everywhere else. Ironically, it is Europe—America's like-minded partner of choice—that is the region most capable to compensate for the limits of the American preponderance and thus moderate its potential for excesses. That, however, cannot be done by any one European state, which might either hope to achieve more influence with closer obedience, *à l'anglaise*, or, conversely, insist that its resistance will translate into more influence, *à la française*. For Europe to exert its weight, its countries must first manage the "finality" they have outlined for their institutions. But how, when, and to what end this daunting task will be completed, if ever, remains unclear: for that task, too, is cause for ambivalence nearly everywhere, especially in Europe itself.

PURPOSE AND COMMITMENT

Americans do not agree with what Europeans view as the worst about America, but on the whole Europeans do like what is best about America—a country that still remains, for many of them, "fable and fact, concrete existence and romance, necessity and imagination."[31] This may be what is most regrettable about the Euro-Atlantic split of the past years—to not have understood, and relied on, Europe's favorable preconception of the United States to sustain the alliance on the eve of the first vital decision of the new century. On either side of the Atlantic, few were those who rose in defense of Al Qaeda's actions, or the Taliban's treatment of women in Afghanistan, or the pervasive brutality that prevailed in Saddam's Iraq, or, most of all, the unbearable threat of a global wave of terror that would spare no one and which no one could therefore afford to neglect. These are the truths that define the purpose of the Alliance; these are "the mystic chords of memory," to return to President Lincoln's eloquent phrase, that cement the alliance's commitment to defending these truths—on behalf of a purpose that remains defined by these shared values. As that purpose was overlooked, the commitments that underwrote it were ignored.

"For centuries," noted de Gaulle during the Cuban missile crisis, Europe was used to "living with threats and menaces" but America "has not had a comparable experience."[32] In the fall of 1962, a lack of consultation did not prevent France (and other countries in Europe) from deferring to President Kennedy's judgment and from pledging full support should "the state of affairs turn from bad to worse." Forty years later, a comparable clash of historic experiences prompted Germany's foreign minister, Joschka Fischer, to observe that "America has not had its Verdun," a laconic reference to wartime conditions in Europe in 1916, when casualties in a matter of minutes on a bad day, day after day, could exceed the losses endured by America on that fateful day in September 2001.[33] But unlike what had been the case forty years earlier, much opposition emerged when the Bush administration again seemed more intent on informing its European allies about decisions it had already made than consulting them before making these decisions. That is not a way to lead an alliance. Partnership is not about deferring to others or being imposed upon by others; it is about making decisions together so that they can also be enforced together and, should there be failure, endured together too.[34] In other words, alliances are about self-denial: to respond to the allies' preferences for action or inaction following consultation that rule against an individual state's preference for the opposite decision, and do so not because going it alone is not an option but because going it together is a better option.

Notwithstanding the partial success of the Iraqi elections held on January 30, 2005, most, if not all, European allies feel less safe now than they were before the war in Iraq started, and many of them attribute their increased vulnerability to a misuse of U.S. military power and a related misunderstanding of the global conflict against terror. That public perception, with potential for considerable resentment and anger, is not limited to countries whose governments actively opposed the war (including France and Germany). It also extends to countries that hardly aspire to more distance from the United States, including Great Britain and Italy. For the Europeans to regain confidence in U.S. intentions and leadership, and restore their faith in the reliability or efficacy of U.S. power, will not be easy. Left unchecked, the credibility gaps opened across the Atlantic, but also within Europe, in and over Iraq will prevent future initiatives with the European allies that would be pursued with all of them as part of a cohesive alliance rather than one national capital at a time as part of a smaller coalition.

In 2004, even countries closely supportive of the Bush administration felt humiliated by the public style of its leadership: haughty, dismissive, unsympathetic, unresponsive, and ultimately unrewarding. But that was not an American failing only. In Europe, too, everyone played a part in making the Atlantic crisis worse than it needed to be—heads of state and government and their senior representatives, elected political leaders, ambassadors and their staffs, journalists and scholars, and other persons of influence. Throughout, Europe's claims for recognition seemed to be elevated into a principle that defines Europe in opposition to, or at the expense of, the United States. Nor was Europe's attitude any more cooperative as some of its political leaders appeared to dismiss their senior partner across the Atlantic as the country of "provincials—marginal, borderland people" it used to be when it was said to stand at the margins of eighteenth-century Euro-American civilization from which the Founding Fathers came.[35] In early 2003, some of the allies, especially France and Belgium but also Germany, misplayed their trump card, namely a legitimate claim that a large majority of their people opposed war: what possibly started as domestic policy with many fundamental implications for foreign policy became, perhaps unexpectedly, foreign policy with some serious domestic implications. Other countries like Spain, Poland, and Italy relied on their closer relations with the United States to reinforce their own leverage within the EU relative to France and Germany: what started mainly as EU policy with consequences for NATO (and thus the United States) became a policy toward the United States (and thus NATO) with consequences for Europe. Such confusion helped neither the EU nor NATO or, as was seen subsequently, their members' heads of state and government.

As compared to past crises, an especially striking feature of the crisis over Iraq was the absence of effective private and public diplomacy.[36] Compared to the other existential crisis lived forty years earlier, the like of Dean Acheson was not sent to European capitals to explain the U.S. president's decisions, and the like of de Gaulle was not there to receive the U.S. president's emissary. On January 30, 2005, as the crisis was running out of control, a joint letter of support signed by the leaders of eight

European countries, including three candidates for EU membership, stated little that could not have been endorsed by all other EU members, if asked and if, that is, the real objective had been to unite rather than to divide the allies. Even for France and Germany, calling for "a united response from the community of democracies" to "the clear and present danger posed by Saddam Hussein's regime" was not objectionable so long as the meaning of "present" (when?), "response" (how?), and "united" (who?) was blurred—which it was. Indeed, notwithstanding such grand statement of intent, the uneven participation of these countries to both combat and post-combat operations confirmed their own divisions over their willingness but also their ability to provide capabilities as a concrete measure of their solidarity. While adding little to NATO strength and solidarity, this letter did much damage to EU cohesion and to these countries' role in Europe. But so did the response of those in Europe who, like French President Jacques Chirac, questioned these countries' right to state their views on issues of vital security concern to them—with implicit warnings of costly reprisals within the then-ongoing negotiations for EU membership.[37]

Just as America must come to a better appreciation of the conditions that move Europe's request for a more effective voice within the Alliance, Europe, too, must reflect on the reasons why America accumulates more power on behalf of the Alliance, pending its allies' acquisition of additional capabilities of their own.[38] In the absence of that mutual awareness of, and respect for, each other, the transatlantic dialogue evolves primarily around what the United States proposes and achieves, which is questioned in Europe, and hardly ever over what the European allies can offer and contribute, which is dismissed in the United States. Admittedly, Europe needs to be needed as the Union it has come to form and for the power it can already contribute. But America, too, wants to be wanted— not only passively until its policies have worked, but actively while obstacles are overcome before success is confirmed. Lacking such mutual reassurances, America's imperial position is assumed by default. The temptation to hang on to that position would be less pronounced if only more Americans could see a viable alternative, as the United Kingdom did after 1945, when its withdrawal from empire was eased by the U.S. readiness and willingness to take its place. But with Europe pretending it is not heard, while America insists that it is not understood, both act and react as if they intended to go their own way even though that is not their intent and is not in their interest.

Even as NATO seems to be losing some of its appeal in the United States, most Americans still favor steps designed to make it stronger and more cohesive.[39] Thinking about America without the institutional access to Europe it provides, and viewing the Atlantic Alliance as a "coalition" like any other, is to imagine an isolated America adrift in an increasingly hostile world—a power whose capabilities would keep it without credible peers, but one whose temperament would also leave it without permanent allies. This is not a happy thought. Nor is it better to think of an America that would escape isolation by returning to variable patterns of bilateral relations with single European states or small coalitions of European countries (as was attempted, ineffectively, in 2003 and continued, to an extent, in 2004). That approach would not be helpful to the United States because it is destructive of the EU, which several of its members—and not only the United Kingdom—still find dependent on benign U.S. support for legitimacy. An institutional fragmentation of the EU would not be a happy outcome either. For thinking about Europe without the EU—or without NATO—is to imagine the kind of Europe that the United States had hoped to end over the past fifty years: unsafe without its American security blanket and astray without its European anchor, older because it would be resurrecting its past and more dangerous because it would be more divided and less predictable.

For the United States and the states of Europe to continue to assert the compatibility of their purpose, as well as the complementarity of their commitments to both the EU and NATO, is a matter of common sense. Neither institution would have been started without the other, each helped the other meet and even exceed the expectations that had given them birth, and both are needed for a whole and free Europe to emerge within a strong and cohesive alliance that benefits all of its members, including the United States. Europe's remarkable transformation into an increasingly cohesive, but still unfinished, union of states is not questioned. Nor is the fact that this transformation was also of considerable benefit to U.S. interests. Whatever the differences between the United States and the European allies, individually or collectively, these differences are less than their respective differences with other parts of the world. Indeed, few issues in the world cannot be addressed more effectively, more expeditiously, and at a lesser cost when the United States and Europe are in agreement than when they are divided.

Admittedly, these conclusions are not self-evident in all instances. There will be cases when a good American (or European) idea, especially about security, will not be equally good for those in Europe (or the United States) who may have to endure its consequences. Nevertheless, for reasons of values, interests, and goals, as well as on grounds of power and influence, the logic of unity transcends the logic of cleavage, and whenever the latter seems to prevail on a specific issue, it cannot be allowed to spread to the others. For Europe, this means that its longing for a compassionate America is an inducement for an American strategy of restraint that would serve both sides of the Atlantic well; for America, this means that its hopes for a stronger, larger, and more united Europe is also compatible with a more active role of Europe in the world, which would also serve both sides of the Atlantic well.

In support of this logic, Europeans ought to do more to reassure Americans that the Union they are completing will continue to make the United States feel at home in Europe. More should be done, for example, to explain, as well as to respond to, the U.S. interests at stake in Europe's quest for the modalities that will permit its institutional finality, and more should be done, too, to enable the United States to state its views about these modalities without leading some EU members to question its supposedly hidden motives. In short, it is time for Europe and the United States to expand to the EU more of the intimacy they already share within NATO, notwithstanding the fact that the United States neither is, wishes to be, or can become a member of a union that is, wishes to be, and ought to remain European. To repeat, America was not born into the world to become a global European Empire, or even, more modestly, an empire in parts of Europe. Concomitantly, however, Europe is not being reborn as a union to deny, let alone defeat, a global American preponderance that the United States does not seek, or even, more modestly, to roll back an American presence in Europe that most Europeans do not deplore. For a nation at the peak of its power, the short-term satisfactions of unilateralism may be more difficult to resist than the long-term obligations of multilateralism. That is a risk. But for a continent on the eve of renewal, a successful challenge to the United States, and the security it conveys, may have short-term pleasures that will not outlast the long-term responsibilities that would inevitably follow. That may be an even bigger risk.

There is some truth to the European fear that Americans may ultimately grow wary of the post–Cold War world, thereby leaving behind a series of conflicts that the Bush administration would have started but which future U.S. administrations would not be willing or able to end. Looming ahead, past Iraq and through what might follow in Iran and elsewhere, there may be emerging a "clash of civilizations" that Americans do not fully understand historically and which America may not fear with the same intensity as in other parts of the world, where cultural tensions have been a permanent dimension of their geography no less than of their history. These apprehensions—about the stamina of American power, but also the prudence of U.S. leadership—are warranted, but they remain premature: as President Bush begins his second term in office, it is simply too early to tell. Still, one thing is clear: forget about isolationism and all that—the know-nothings of yesteryear know better now, and there is no coming back from a world that has found its place in America even as America still struggles to define its role in the world.[40] In the post-9/11 world, there is little room for lasting indifference or moral ambiguity. In short, Americans will do what is needed and as long as it is needed so long as they are told what it takes, why, and to what ends.

But will the European allies, and if so, how? Notwithstanding the shortcomings of the Bush administration in Iraq, however these shortcomings are understood, and granted the many questions raised about Europe's reliability in the war on terror, however these questions are phrased, the future of the Euro-Atlantic partnership is not self-evident. What seems self-evident, however, is that there has to be some order out there, and that while any future world order will be significantly shaped by the availability of American power, that power alone will not be as effective and as durable in the absence of willing, capable, and relevant allies. Most of these are found in the like-minded and increasingly look-alike continent that lies across the Atlantic. Without these allies, and without the vital partnership we have come to form with them, the United States would soon grow weary of the role it assumed in the fall of 2001, in a legitimate burst of emotional outrage and national anger subsequently sustained by the elementary imperative of self-defense and self-preservation.

NOTES

INTRODUCTION

1. See, by the author, *Memories of Europe's Future, Farewell to Yesteryear* (Washington, D.C.: CSIS Press, 1999), p. 11.

2. As written by Will and Ariel Durant, "The present is the past rolled up for action" while "the past is the present unrolled for understanding." Will and Ariel Durant, *The Story of Civilization*, vol. VI, *The Reformation* (New York: Simon & Schuster, 1935), p. 2. According to Immanuel Wallerstein, a different sort of historian, "History can only be written about the present and the future. We are speaking to the metaphysical question, where are we? We are writing of the present . . . where will we be? And where would be like to be?" *Geopolitics and Culture: Essays on the Changing World-System* (Cambridge: Cambridge University Press, 1991), pp. 1–15.

3. Charles Kupchan, *The End of the American Era: U.S. Foreign Policy and the Geopolitics of the Twenty-First Century* (New York: Alfred A. Knopf, 2002), p. 205.

4. As noted more than a decade ago by Richard J. Kerry, Senator John F. Kerry's father, "What the Kennedy and Johnson administrations saw in Vietnam bore little relation to reality. . . . [There] escalation depended on a frame of mind. It was irreversible only as long as that frame of mind lasted." Richard J. Kerry, *The Star-Spangled Mirror: America's Image of Itself and the World* (Savage, Md.: Rowman & Littlefield Publishers, 1990), pp. 39–45.

5. The conclusions of *The 9/11 Commission Report* are unequivocal: "To date, we have seen no evidence . . . indicating that Iraq cooperated with al Qaeda in developing or carrying out any attacks against the United States." *The 9/11 Commission Report* (New York: W.W. Norton & Company, 2004), p. 66.

6. These are the same two "propositions" then-Secretary of Defense Robert McNamara urged President Kennedy "to accept as foundations for . . . further thinking" at the start of the thirteen-day Cuban missile crisis. Ernest R. May and Philip D. Zelikow, eds., *The Kennedy Tapes: Inside the White House during the Cuban Missile Crisis* (Cambridge, Mass.: Harvard University Press, 1997), p. 57.

7. Henry A. Kissinger, "America's Assignment," *Newsweek*, November 8, 2004, p. 41.

8. Alan Milward, *The European Rescue of the Nation-State*, 2nd ed. (London: Routledge, 2000), and Desmond Dinan, *Europe Recast: A History of European Union* (Boulder, Colo.: Lynne Rienner, 2004).

9. Raymond Aron, "Nations et empires," in *Encyclopédie française* (Paris: Société nouvelle de l'Encyclopédie française, 1957), vol. II, *La vie internationale*. Reproduced in *The Dawn of Universal History: Selected Essays from a Witness to the Twentieth Century*, translated by Barbara Bray (New York: Basic Books, 2002), p. 4.

10. In 2004, "the eurozone's growth rate will be half that of the US and Japan. In the last three years [2001–2003]," he adds, "cumulative eurozone growth has been just 3 per cent . . . compared with 5.5 per cent in the US and 6 in the UK." Gordon Brown, "Europe Must Meet the Challenge of Reform," *Financial Times*, September 10, 2004.

11. See Ulrike Guérot, "The European Paradox: Widening and Deepening in the European Union," *U.S.-Europe Analysis Series*, Brookings Institution, June 2004.

12. Ronald D. Asmus, James Dobbins, and John Hulsman, *One Year On: Lessons from Iraq*, Chaillot paper, no. 68 (Paris: Institute for Security Studies, March 2004), pp. 169–77.

13. Judy Dempsey, "NATO Must Modernize and Rethink Its Strategy," *Financial Times*, June 25, 2004, p. 11.

14. Seven of the twenty-six NATO members are not in the EU (Bulgaria, Iceland, Norway, Romania, and Turkey, in addition to the United States and Canada) and six EU members are not in NATO (Austria, Cyprus, Finland, Ireland, Malta, and Sweden).

CHAPTER 1

1. George F. Kennan, "Putting History at Risk," *New York Times*, May 27, 1984.

2. Hannah Arendt, *The Origins of Totalitarianism* (San Diego: Harcourt, Inc. 1995), p. vii.

3. John Keegan, *The First World War* (New York: Vintage Books, 1998), p. 3.

4. According to Theodore White, *Fire in the Ashes: Europe in the Mid-Century* (New York: William Sloane Associates, 1953), p. 384.

5. Stefan Zweig, *The World of Yesterday* (London: University of Nebraska Press, 1964), p. xx.

6. Dominique de Villepin, *Le requin et la mouette* (Paris: Plon, 2004), p. 76.

7. Eric Hobsbawm, in conversation with Antonio Polito, *The New Century* (London: Little, Brown, 2000), p. 62. For Zbigniew Brzezinski, globalization—a "buzzword"—has come "to signify the onset of a novel age of world-wide accountability, transparency, and cooperation." *The Choice: Global Domination or Global Leadership* (New York: Basic Books, 2004), p. 139.

8. George Soros, *The Bubble of American Supremacy: The Costs of Bush's War in Iraq* (New York: Public Affairs, 2004).

9. George Liska, *Imperial America* (Baltimore: Johns Hopkins University Press, 1967), p. 9. Also, by the same author, *War and Order: Reflections on Vietnam and History* (Baltimore: Johns Hopkins University Press, 1968).

10. John Lewis Gaddis, *We Now Know: Rethinking Cold War History* (Oxford, U.K.: Clarendon Press, 1997), p. 27. For an earlier discussion, see Ronald Steel, *Pax Americana* (New York: Viking Press, 1967), pp. 15–27.

11. Hubert Védrine, with Dominique Moisi, *France in an Age of Globalization*, translated by Philip H. Gordon (Washington, D.C.: Brookings Institution, 2001), p. 44.

12. Niall Ferguson, *Empire: The Rise and Demise of the British World Order and the Lessons for Global Power* (New York: Basic Books, 2003), p. 370. Also, by the same author, *Colossus: The Price of America's Empire* (New York: Penguin, 2004), pp. 6, 78.

13. Arthur Schlesinger Jr., "The Making of a Mess," *New York Review of Books*, vol. 51, no. 14 (September 23, 2004).

14. Quoted by Bob Woodward, *Bush at War* (New York: Simon & Schuster, 2002), pp. 332–34.

15. James Kurth, "The Adolescent Empire," *National Interest* 48 (Summer 1997): 3–15.

16. Robert Jervis, "The Compulsive Empire," *Foreign Policy* 137 (July/August 2003): 83–87.

17. Robert Kagan, "The Benevolent Empire," *Foreign Policy* 112 (Summer 1998): 24–35.

18. Mark Hertsgaard, *The Eagle's Shadow* (New York: Farrar, Straus and Giroux, 2002), pp. 66ff.

19. See William E. Odom and Robert Dujarric, *America's Inadvertent Empire* (New Haven, Conn.: Yale University Press, 2004).

20. See Michael Ignatieff, *Empire Lite: Nation-Building in Bosnia, Kosovo, and Afghanistan* (New York: Penguin, 2003).

21. Jim Garrison, *America as Empire: Global Leader or Rogue Power* (San Francisco: Berrett-Koehler Publishers, 2002), p. 166.

22. Quoted in Norman A. Graebner, *The New Isolationism: A Study in Politics and Foreign Policy since 1950* (New York: Ronald Press Co., 1956), p. 6.

23. Robert W. Tucker, *The Inequality of Nations* (New York: Basic Books, 1977), p. 28.

24. Charles Krauthammer, "Democratic Realism: An American Foreign Policy for a Unipolar World," 2004 Irving Kristol Lecture, Washington, D.C., American Enterprise Institute, February 10, 2004.

25. Joseph S. Nye Jr., *Bound to Lead: The Changing Nature of American Power* (New York: Basic Books, 1990), and *The Paradox of American Power* (New York: Oxford University Press, 2002).

26. For an argument that "Europe [will] catch up with America soon," see Charles Kupchan, *The End of the American Era*, op. cit., p. 119.

27. John Rossant, "How Europe Could Grow Again," *Business Week*, International Editions, November 17, 2003, p. 46 ff.

28. Unsigned editorial, "Europe vs. America," *Wall Street Journal*, June 18, 2004, p. 10.

29. Richard Rosecrance, "Croesus and Caesar: The Essential Transatlantic Symbiosis," *National Interest*, no. 72 (Summer 2003): 31–34.

30. Felix Rohatyn, "The Unbearable Expense of Global Dominance," *Financial Times*, June 10, 2003, p. 13.

31. Harold James, "Lessons to Learn from the Decline and Fall of Empire," *Financial Times*, December 30, 2002, p. 15.

32. Niall Ferguson, *Colossus*, op. cit., p. 73.

33. George Packer, "Efforts Begin to Mend France's Loss of Self-Confidence in Brave New Europe," *Financial Times*, September 22, 2004.

34. Sophie Meunier, "The French Exception," *Foreign Affairs* 79, no. 4 (July/August 2000): 104–16.

35. See the excellent account by James Mann, *The Rise of the Vulcans: The History of Bush's War Cabinet* (New York: Viking Press, 2004), pp. xiii–xiv, 137.

36. As was written of the U.S. intervention in World War I, in "Twilight of Idols," in *The World of Randolph Bourne*, edited by Lillian Schlossel (New York: E. P. Dutton & Co., 1965), pp. 198–99.

37. Walter Laqueur, "America and the World: The Next Four Years," *Commentary* 63 (March 1977): 35. Also, Norman Podhoretz, *Present Danger* (New York: Simon and Schuster, 1980), p. 83.

38. Paul Wolfowitz, quoted in James Mann, *Rise of the Vulcans*, op. cit., p. 81.

39. See David Gelernter, "The Roots of European Appeasement," *Weekly Standard* 8, no. 2 (September 23, 2002).

40. Senator John F. Kerry's acceptance speech at the Democratic Convention, on July 29, 2004. Also, Robert Kagan, "The Reagan Doctrine," *Washington Post*, August 1, 2004.

41. For a detailed account of the debate at the League of Nations, see George Scott, *The Rise and Fall of the League of Nations* (New York: Macmillan Publishing Co., 1974), pp. 94–97 and passim.

42. The League's failure was less due to the U.S. failure to ratify than to Europe's failure to build it. The verdict should by now be clear: "Everything we know about the history and the nature of international relations goes to show that the League, as it was constructed, was bound to fail." F. H. Hinsley, *Power and the Pursuit of Peace* (London: Cambridge University Press, 1963), p. 309.

43. Conan Fischer, *The Ruhr Crisis, 1923–1924* (Oxford: Oxford University Press, 2003), p. 290.

44. Quoted in Selig Adler, *The Isolationist Impulse: Its Twentieth-Century Reaction* (New York: Free Press, 1957), p. 144.

45. For a discussion of the "might-have-beens" of Weimar Germany, turn to Anton W. de Porte, *Europe between the Superpowers: The Enduring Balance* (New Haven, Conn.: Yale University Press, 2nd edition, 1986), pp. 32–41.

46. An instructive transcript of these discussions is provided in Ernest May and Philip Zelikow, *The Kennedy Tapes: Inside the White House during the Cuban Missile Crisis*, op. cit. The quotes listed here appear on pp. 84 and 65–66. Inter-allied tensions over relations with Cuba made Kennedy reluctant to consult until he had decided to institute the quarantine.

47. According to *Oral History with Dean Acheson*, April 27, 1964. Quoted by Thomas Risse-Kappen, *Cooperation among Democracies: The European Influence on U.S. Foreign Policy* (Princeton, N.J.: Princeton University Press, 1995), p. 157.

48. *The National Security Strategy of the United States of America* (Washington, D.C., September 2002), pp. 14–15.

49. Ronald D. Asmus, James Dobbins, and John Hulsman, *One Year On: Lessons from Iraq*, op. cit., p. 149.

50. Michael M. Harrison, *The Reluctant Ally: France and Atlantic Security* (Baltimore: Johns Hopkins University Press, 1981), p. 59.

51. Philip Zelikow and Condoleezza Rice, *Germany Unified and Europe Transformed: A Study in Statecraft* (Cambridge, Mass.: Harvard University Press, 1995), p. 169.

52. George Kennan, quoted in Wilson D. Miscamble, *George F. Kennan and the Making of American Foreign Policy, 1947–1950* (Princeton, N.J.: Princeton University Press, 1992), p. 117.

53. Dean Acheson, *Present at the Creation: My Years at the State Department* (New York: Norton, 1969), pp. 457–59.

54. De Gaulle, quoted in Geoffrey Warner, "Why the General Said No," *International Affairs* 78, no. 4 (2002): 876. See also, André Passeron, *De Gaulle Parle, 1962–1966* (Paris: Fayard, 1966), pp. 199–207, and Harold Macmillan, *At the End of the Day, 1961–1963* (New York: Harper & Row, 1973), p. 348.

55. Prime Minister's Speech to the Stock Exchange, Warsaw, Poland, October 6, 2000.

56. Speech by President Jacques Chirac for the twentieth anniversary of the Institut Français des Relations Internationales, Paris, Elysée Palace, November 4, 1999.

57. Remarks by Dr. Condoleezza Rice at the International Institute for Strategic Studies, London, June 26, 2003.

58. Quoted by Jim Hoagland, "Chirac's 'Multipolar World,'" *Washington Post*, February 4, 2004.

59. Quoted in Alain Peyrefitte, *C'était de Gaulle* (Paris: Fayard, 2000), p. 145.

60. Discours d'ouverture de M. Dominique de Villepin, Onzième conference des ambassadeurs, Paris, August 28, 2003.

CHAPTER 2

1. Dean Acheson, *Present at the Creation*, op. cit., p. xvii.

2. Reinhold Niebuhr, "The Foreign Policy of American Conservatism and Liberalism," in *Christian Realism and Political Problems*, edited by Reinhold Niebuhr (New York: Scribner's, 1953), pp. 58-64.

3. Walter Lippmann, *The Cold War: A Study in U.S. Foreign Policy* (New York: Harper & Row, 1947), pp. 21-23.

4. Thomas Donnelly, "Learning to Live without Europe," *National Security Outlook*, American Enterprise Institute, May 2004.

5. Samuel P. Huntington, *The Clash of Civilizations and the Remaking of World Order* (New York: Simon & Schuster, 1996), p. 21.

6. Robert Kagan, *Of Paradise and Power: America and Europe in the New World Order* (New York: Vintage Books, 2004), p. 107.

7. David McCullough, *Truman* (New York: Simon & Schuster, 1992), pp. 349, 352, 525.

8. Henry Kissinger, *Does America Need a Foreign Policy? Toward a Diplomacy for the 21st Century* (New York: Simon & Schuster, 2001), p. 33.

9. Charles A. Kupchan, "The End of the West," *The Atlantic Monthly* 290, no. 4 (November 2002): 42-44.

10. François Heisbourg vs. Charles Grant, "How Should Europe Respond to the New America," *Prospect Magazine* (April 2003): 16-20.

11. François Heisbourg, "*Accablant 6 juin 2004*," *Le Monde*, June 5, 2004.

12. Secretary Shultz is quoted in James Harding, "George Shultz Still Holds Sway in the Corridors of Power," *Financial Times*, November 11, 2001.

13. David P. Calleo, *The Atlantic Fantasy: The U.S., NATO, and Europe* (Baltimore: Johns Hopkins University Press, 1970), and *Beyond American*

Hegemony: The Future of the Western Alliance (New York: Basic Books, 1987), pp. 3–4.

14. Ronald Steel, *The End of Alliances: America and the Future of Europe* (New York: Viking Press, 1964), pp. 4–5 and 80.

15. Joseph S. Nye Jr., *The Paradox of American Power*, op. cit., p. 29. Professor Nye had been more skeptical in 1990, when he still questioned "the exaggerated Euro-optimism for 1992. . . . If European unity remains elusive, then speculation about Europe as the leading power in the twenty-first century is exaggerated." *Bound to Lead*, op. cit., p. 154.

16. Charles A. Kupchan, "The Last Days of the Alliance," *Financial Times*, November 17, 2002.

17. Christopher Layne, "America as European Hegemon," *National Interest*, no. 72 (Summer 2003): 28.

18. Thomas Freedman, "I Love the E.U.," *New York Times*, June 22, 2001. Compare this sudden burst of enthusiasm for the EU with a later column, "Our War with France," *New York Times*, September 19, 2003.

19. Samuel P. Huntington, "The U.S.—Decline or Renewal?" *Foreign Affairs* (Winter 1988–89): 93. See also, Simon Serfaty, *Taking Europe Seriously* (New York: St. Martin's Press, 1992).

20. Walter Russell Mead, *Special Providence: American Foreign Policy and How It Changed the World* (New York: Alfred A. Knopf, 2001), p. 30.

21. Andrew Sullivan in "Friends? Foes? Disconnected Strangers? Europe and America over the Next Generation," a symposium with Jeffrey Gedmin, Andrew Sullivan, Jonathan Rauch, Mark Steyn, Michael Kelly, Jonah Goldberg, and John O' Sullivan, *American Enterprise* 13, no. 8 (December 2002): 30–35.

22. Richard Perle is quoted by Edward Pilkington and Ewen MacAskill, "Europe Lacks Moral Fibre," *Guardian* (London), November 13, 2002.

23. Richard Perle, "The State of the Euro-Atlantic Partnership," Trilateral Commission, 26th European Meeting, Prague, October 28–29, 2002.

24. See Lee Harris, "The Intellectual Origins of America-Bashing," *Policy Review*, no. 116 (December 2002/January 2003): 1–11.

25. See William A. Williams, *The Tragedy of American History* (New York: Delta Publishing, 1959).

26. Attributed to historian Peter Gray by David Gelernter, "The Roots of European Appeasement," op. cit., p. 19.

27. Stuart Reid, "The Anti-Europeans," *American Conservative*, January 27, 2003.

28. Niall Ferguson, "Europe's Response to Iraq Reflects an Old Rift," *New York Times*, February 23, 2003.

29. David Reynolds, "1940: Fulcrum of the Twentieth Century?" *International Affairs* 66, no. 2 (1990): 327–29. See also Jean Pierre Azéma, *1940, l'année terrible* (Paris: Editions du Seuil, 1990), and Andrew Shennan, *The Fall of France, 1940* (London: Pearson Education, 2000).

30. The question of war debts had disastrous consequences on European countries where the United States was promptly cast in "a Shylock role." In late 1932, Britain paid up in full, but not without a bitterness that led some members of the government to urge payment in silver—Judas-like. In 1933, the French led the defaulters in a "spectacular battle" for which, according to Cordell Hull, "the dictator nations occupied first-row seats," including Germany, the earlier beneficiary, in 1931, of a U.S.-inspired moratorium on the repayment of its own war debts. See George Scott, op. cit., pp. 254–56.

31. Alfred Vagts, "Battle and Other Combatant Casualties in the Second World War," *Journal of Politics* 7, no. 3 (1945): 285.

32. Charles Krauthammer, "Europe and 'Those People,'" *Washington Post*, April 26, 2002.

33. George Will, "Final Solution, Phase 2," *Washington Post*, May 2, 2002.

34. *American Spectator*, June 2002.

35. Karl Zinsmeister, "Old and In the Way," *American Enterprise* 13, no. 8 (December 2002), p. 9.

36. Charles Krauthammer, "U.S. Power Rises as NATO Fades into Irrelevance," *Washington Post*, May 27, 2002.

37. Cited by John Harper, "American Visions of Europe after 1989," in *Visions of America and Europe: September 11, Iraq, and Transatlantic Relations*, edited by Christina Balis and Simon Serfaty (Washington, D.C.: CSIS Press, 2004), p. 38.

38. Jeff Gedmin, "The Alliance Is Doomed," *Washington Post*, May 20, 2002.

39. Simon Schama, "The Unloved American," *New Yorker* 79, no. 3 (March 10, 2003): 34.

40. Vincent Auriol, *Mon Septennat, 1947–1954* (Paris: Gallimard, 1970). Quoted in Alfred Grosser, *Les Occidentaux* (Paris: Fayard, 1978), p. 139.

41. François Mitterrand, *Ici et maintenant* (Paris: Fayard, 1980), pp. 231, 242.

42. Mitterrand's appraisal of Reagan was shared with Helmut Kohl, as reported by Mitterrand's close associate Jacques Attali. Quoted in Harvey Sicherman, "Where's the Rest of Me?" *Orbis* 44, no. 3 (Summer 2000): 482.

43. Special report, unsigned, "Does Britain Like Us? Anti-Americanism Is Growing . . . Fed by Fear, Envy, Frustration, and Years of Want," *Newsweek* (December 22, 1947), pp. 26–27.

44. Denis W. Brogan, *The American Character* (New York: Time Inc. Book Division, 1962), introduction to the Vintage edition 1956, p. xxvii.

45. Stanley Hoffmann, "To Be or Not To Be French," in *Ideas and Ideals: Essays on Politics in Honor of Stanley Hoffmann*, edited by Linda B. Miller and Michael J. Smith (Boulder, Colo.: Westview Press, 1993), p. 32.

46. Norman Podhoretz, *Making It* (New York: Random House, 1967), p. 85.

47. Will Hutton, *The World We're In* (Boston: Little, Brown, 2002), p. 357.

48. "Put bluntly," noted Richard Perle, "I believe the French policy is to diminish American influence in Europe and throughout the world." Quoted in James Kitfield, "Fractured Alliances," *National Journal*, March 8, 2003. See the author's *La France vue d'Amérique: Réflexions sur la francophobie à Washington* (Paris: IFRI, 2002).

49. See W.G. Sebald, *On the Natural History of Destruction*, translated by Anthea Bell (New York: Modern Library, 1999), pp. 3–4 and 12.

50. Bernard-Henry Lévy, "Anti-Americanism in the Old Europe," *NPQ* 20, no. 2, Spring 2003.

51. The German Marshall Fund of the United States and the Compagnia di San Paolo, *Transatlantic Trends, 2004*, pp. 11–12.

52. Jean-François Revel, *L'obsession anti-américaine* (Paris: Plon, 2002). Also, by the author, "A Dialogue of the Deaf," *Aspenia*, nos. 19–20 (2003): 69–80.

53. Amitai Etzioni, *The Monochrome Society* (Princeton, N.J.: Princeton University Press, 2001), p. xiv.

54. See, for example, Michael Howard, "Mistake to Declare This a War?" *RUSI Journal* 146 (December 2001): 1–4. Also, Eliot A. Cohen, "A Strange War," *National Interest*, no. 65 (Thanksgiving 2001): 11–23.

55. The phrase was first used by Vice President Richard Cheney, who feared that September 11 might "become a permanent feature in our kind of way of life." Quoted in Bob Woodward, "CIA Told to Do Whatever Necessary to Kill bin Laden," *Washington Post*, October 21, 2001, p. A22.

56. For example, Alain Frachon, "Les années bis," *Le Monde*, February 16, 2002.

57. A full transcript of President George W. Bush's news conference, from which these statements are excerpted, appeared in the *Washington Post*, October 12, 2001.

58. President George W. Bush, cited by Bob Woodward, *Bush At War* (New York: Simon & Schuster, 2002), p. 96.

59. President George W. Bush's remarks to the New York Police Department Command and Control Center Personnel, New York, February 6, 2002.

60. Bob Woodward, *Plan of Attack*, op. cit., p. 28.

61. President George W. Bush quoted in the *Washington Post*, January 27, 2002.

62. George Packer, "War after the War," *New Yorker*, November 24, 2003, p. 62.

63. President George W. Bush, Speech at the American Enterprise Institute, Washington, D.C., February 26, 2003.

CHAPTER 3

1. Raymond Aron, *The Century of Total War* (Garden City, N.Y.: Doubleday, 1954), p. 301.

2. Alan Milward, *The European Rescue of the Nation-State*, op. cit., pp. 327–28.

3. Jean Monnet, according to Paul-Henry Spaak, *The Continuing Battle: Memoirs of a European* (London: George Weidenfeld and Nicolson, 1971), pp. 213–14.

4. Dean Acheson, *Present at the Creation*, op. cit., pp. 76–77.

5. U.S. Ambassador to France, David Bruce, as quoted by Dean Acheson, *Present at the Creation*, op. cit., p. 382.

6. Desmond Dinan, *Europe Recast*, op. cit., pp. 36–37.

7. Konrad Adenauer, as assessed by Gordon A. Craig, *The Germans* (New York: Meridian Book, 1982), p. 47.

8. "The adoption in Europe of the American system of union" in Germany, declared President Ulysses Grant in 1871, "under the control and the direction of a free people educated to self-restraint, cannot fail to extend popular institutions and to enlarge the peaceful influence of American ideas." Quoted by Detlef Junker, *The Manichean Trap: American Perceptions of the German Empire, 1871–1945*, German Historical Institute, Occasional Papers, No. 12 (1995), p. 12.

9. G. John Ikenberry, "Rethinking the Origins of American Hegemony," in *American Foreign Policy: Theoretical Essays*, edited by G. J. Ikenberry (New York: Longman, 2005, 5th edition), pp. 111–35.

10. Georges-Henri Soutou, "France," in *The Origins of the Cold War in Europe: International Perspectives,* edited by David Reynolds (New Haven, Conn.: Yale University Press, 1994), pp. 103–4.

11. Robert W. Tucker, *Nation or Empire?* (Baltimore: Johns Hopkins University Press, 1968), p. 6.

12. Henry Kissinger in Richard Pfeffer ed., *No More Vietnams? The War and the Future of American Foreign Policy* (New York: Harper & Row, 1968), p. 13.

13. The theme is developed at greater length in Simon Serfaty, "No More Dissent," *Foreign Policy* 11 (Summer 1973): 144–58.

14. George Liska, *Imperial America*, op. cit., pp. 108–9.

15. Seyom Brown, *The Crises of Power: An Interpretation of United States Foreign Policy during the Kissinger Years* (New York: Columbia University Press, 1979), p. 144.

16. George Liska, *Beyond Kissinger: Way of Conservative Statecraft* (Baltimore: Johns Hopkins University Press, 1975), p. 6.

17. Henry Kissinger, *A World Restored* (Boston: Houghton Mifflin, 1973), p. 320.

18. President Jimmy Carter is quoted in Gaddis Smith, *Morality, Reason and Power: American Diplomacy in the Carter Years* (New York: Hill and Wang, 1986), p. 28. "To me," reflected Carter, "moral principles were the best foundation for the exertion of American power and influence." Jimmy Carter, *Keeping Faith: Memoirs of a President* (New York: Bantam Books, 1982), p. 143.

19. Richard Pipes, "Misinterpreting the Cold War: The Hardliners Had It Right," *Foreign Affairs* 73, no. 1 (January–February 1994): 157.

20. Robert Jervis, "Mission Impossible: Creating a Grand Strategy," in *The New American Interventionism: Lessons from Successes and Failures*, edited by Demetrios James Caraley (New York: Columbia University Press, 1999), p. 206.

21. Richard Haass is quoted in Nicholas Lemann, "The Next World Order," *New Yorker* (April 1, 2002): 45.

22. Richard Holbrooke, *To End a War* (New York: Random House, 1998), p. 21.

23. Madeleine Albright, *Madam Secretary* (New York: Miramax Books, 2003), pp. 189–90.

24. Theodore White, *In Search of History: A Personal Adventure* (New York: Warner Books, 1978), p. 275.

25. As noted by Holbrooke, op. cit., p. 22. The book in question was Robert D. Kaplan, *Balkan Ghosts: A Journey through History* (New York: Vintage Books, 1993).

26. Wesley K. Clark, *Waging Modern War: Bosnia, Kosovo, and the Future of Combat* (New York: Public Affairs, 2001), p. 59.

27. Albright, *Madam Secretary*, op. cit., p. 265.

28. Holbrooke, *To End a War*, op. cit., pp. 205 and 233.

29. David Armstrong, "Dick Cheney's Song of America," *Harper's Magazine* (October 2002): 76–83.

30. Benjamin Schwartz and Christopher Layne, "A New Grand Strategy," *Atlantic Monthly* 289, issue 1 (January 2002): 36–42. See also, James Mann, *Rise of the Vulcans*, op. cit., pp. 198–215.

31. Donald Rumsfeld, "The Coalition and the Mission," *Washington Post*, October 21, 2001.

32. Julian Lindley-French, *Terms of Engagement: The Paradox of American Power and the Transatlantic Dilemma, Post-11 September*, Chaillot Papers, no. 52, Institute for Security Studies (May 2002), p. 11.

33. President George W. Bush, cited by Bob Woodward, *Bush at War*, op. cit., p. 17.

34. Quoted in John F. Harris and Mike Allen, "Series of Misjudgments Cost President His Lead," *Washington Post*, August 29, 2004.

35. President George W. Bush is quoted by Judy Keen, "Bush Commands Attention on Global Stage," *USA Today*, November 25, 2002. "The viewers would like to know more on how [Christ] changed your heart," candidate Bush

was asked during one of the Republican presidential debates in the spring of 2000. "Well," Bush replied, "if they don't know, it's going to be hard to explain."

36. This was also the case for many of the president's main security advisers. Ahmed Chalabi, for example, "won the confidence of the neo-conservatives" because "what he said . . . was undistinguishable from what they believed." Robin Wright, "Standing of Former Key U.S. Ally in Iraq Falls to New Low," *Washington Post*, May 21, 2004.

37. Quoted by Bob Woodward, *Bush At War*, op. cit., p. 341.

38. Henry A. Kissinger, *White House Years*, op. cit., pp. 39–40.

39. Zbigniew Brzezinski, *Power and Principle: Memoir of the National Security Adviser, 1977–1981* (New York: Farrar, Straus, Giroux, 1983), p. 63.

40. "It's always been that combination of power and morality [in Bush] that I've found particularly interesting," notes Condoleezza Rice, to explain her general interests but also, it can be surmised, to describe her personal interest in the president she serves. Quoted in Nicholas Lemann, "Without a Doubt," *New Yorker* (October 14 and 21, 2002): 164–80.

41. Condoleezza Rice, Ibid.

42. Margaret Macmillan, *Paris 1919* (New York, Random House, 2003), p. 3.

43. Edmund Morris, *Dutch: A Memoir of Ronald Reagan* (New York: Random House, 1999), pp. xv and 4.

44. James Chace, *Acheson* (New York: Simon & Schuster, 1998), p. 32.

45. Jacques Andréani, *"Les Européens auront les Américains qu'ils méritent,"* *Commentaire* 94 (Summer 2001), pp. 295–302. One of the more disturbing media "reports" on the 2000 campaign was Philippe Labro's offensive *"Chronique de l'Amérique en campagne,"* *Le Monde*, October 18, 2000, pp. 16–17. According to Labro, then-Governor Bush was a "cretin" and then-Vice President Gore was a "stuck-up."

46. See, for example, Lionel Barber, "Why Clinton Is Giving Europe the Jitters," *Washington Post*, October 24, 1993.

47. For an early analysis of the Clinton legacy, see the author's "Memories of Leadership," *Brown Journal of World Affairs* 5, no. 2 (Summer/Fall 1998): 3–16.

48. Chris Patten, "Europe's Leaders Welcome American Display of Partnership," *International Herald Tribune*, June 19, 2001.

49. Bob Woodward, *Bush at War*, op. cit., p. 39.

50. Robert D. Kaplan, *The Coming Anarchy* (New York: Random House, 2000), p. 24.

51. Bob Woodward, *Bush at War*, op. cit., p. 38.

52. See the author's "Visions of Leadership," op. cit., pp. 3–16.

CHAPTER 4

1. Stefan Zweig, *The World of Yesterday*, op. cit., p. xx.

2. Albert Camus, "Humanity at Zero Hour," quoted in Jeffrey C. Isaac, *Arendt, Camus and Modern Rebellion* (New Haven, Conn.: Yale University Press, 1994), p. 21.

3. Robert Kagan, *Of Paradise and Power*, op. cit., p. 135.

4. Isaiah Berlin, *Four Essays on Liberty* (New York: Oxford University Press, 1969), p. 52.

5. The idea of "synthesis" is borrowed from Friedrich Nietzsche. Quoted in Peter Rietbergen, *Europe: A Cultural History* (London: Routledge: 1998), p. 407.

6. See Simon Serfaty, "American Reflections on Europe's Finality," in *The European Finality Debate and Its National Dimensions*, edited by S. Serfaty (Washington, D.C.: CSIS Press, 2003), pp. 1–20.

7. Edward H. Carr, *Nationalism and After* (London: Macmillan, 1968), p. 9.

8. For a compelling portrait see Luigi Barzini, *The Europeans* (New York: Penguin Books, 1984).

9. "A nation as such is obviously not a empirical thing," wrote Hans Morgenthau. "A nation as such cannot be seen." Hans J. Morgenthau, *Politics among Nations* (New York: Alfred A. Knopf, 1967, 4th edition), p. 97.

10. See Jeremy Rifkin, *The European Dream* (London: Penguin, 2004). Quoted by Andrew Moravcsik, "Europe Is the New Role Model for the World," *Financial Times*, October 6, 2004.

11. For an early and still instructive discussion, see also Leon N. Lindbergh and Stuart A. Scheingold, *Europe's Would-Be Polity: Patterns of Change in the European Community* (Englewood Cliffs, N.J.: Prentice-Hall, 1970), p. 106.

12. Alberta M. Sbragia, "Thinking about the European Future: The Use of Comparison," in *Euro-Politics: Institutions and Policy-Making in the "New"*

European Community, edited by Alberta M. Sbragia (Washington, D.C.: Brookings Institution, 1992), p. 261.

13. Timothy Garton Ash, "The European Orchestra," *New York Review of Books*, May 17, 2001, p. 60.

14. Martin Walker, "What Europeans Think of America," *World Policy Journal* 17, no. 2 (Summer 2000): 26.

15. Jurgen Habermas and Jacques Derrida, "Europe: Plea for a Common Foreign Policy," our translation by Douglas Gillison from its French version, *"Europe: plaidoyer pour une politique extérieure commune," Libération*, June 1, 2003.

16. Arthur N. Holcombe, "An American View of European Union," *American Political Science Review* 46 (1952): 418.

17. Liah Greenfeld, *Nationalism: Five Roads to Modernity* (Cambridge, Mass.: Harvard University Press, 1992), p. 422.

18. Marten van Heuven, "In an Age of American Dominance: Does the Transatlantic Relationship Matter?" (Arlington, Va.: RAND, P-8074, 2003), p. 6.

19. Jack Rakove, "Europe's Floundering Fathers," *Foreign Policy* 138 (September–October 2003): 30.

20. Peter Rietbergen, *Europe: A Cultural History*, op. cit., p. 431.

21. Cited in Nathan Leites, *The Rules of the Game in Paris* (Chicago: University of Chicago Press, 1969), p. 13.

22. Margaret Thatcher in a television interview with David Frost. Quoted in Fred Barbash, "Thatcher's Major Payoff," *Washington Post*, June 15, 1995.

23. The initial six members of the European Economic Community clearly outperformed their counterparts in EFTA both before and after the launch of the Common Market in 1958—the five years before and the seven years after. Leon Lindbergh, op. cit., p. 28.

24. See Simon Serfaty, "The Transatlantic Dimension," in *The Future of Europe: Integration and Enlargement*, edited by Fraser Cameron (London: Routledge, 2004), pp. 135–48.

25. Tariq Ramadan, *To Be a European Muslim* (London: The Islamic Foundation, 1999), p. 1.

26. Shireen Hunter, ed. *Islam: Europe's Second Religion* (Washington, D.C.: CSIS Press, 2002). Also, Robert J. Pauly Jr., *Islam in Europe: Integration or Marginalization* (Burlington, Vt.: Ashgate, 2003).

27. On the eve of the European Commission's report on Turkey's bid for EU membership, a leading commissioner, Fritz Bolkenstein, publicly warned against the ongoing "Islamization" of Europe which, kept unchecked due to demographic and migration trends, would mean that "the liberation of Vienna [from the Turks] would have been in vain." Daniel Dombey and Tobias Buck, "Islamization Warning Clouds Turks' EU Drive," *Financial Times*, September 8, 2001.

28. Bassam Tibi, *The Challenge of Fundamentalism, Political Islam and the New World Disorder* (Berkeley: University of California Press, 1998), p. 18. See also Steven Vertovec and Cery Peach, eds., *Islam in Europe: The Politics of Religion and Community* (New York: St. Martin's Press, 1997), p. 4, and Richard Fletcher, *The Barbarian Conversion: From Paganism to Christianity* (New York: Henry Holt, 1997), p. 304.

29. David Willetts, *Old Europe? Demographic Change and Pension Reform* (London: Centre for European Reform, 2003). See also, United Nations, *World Population Prospects—the 2002 Revision* (2003).

30. Thomas Fuller, "Europe Wants Workers to Move," *International Herald Tribune*, February 13, 2002.

31. Geoffrey Barraclough, *An Introduction to Contemporary History* (Harmondsworth, U.K.: Penguin, 1967), p. 77.

32. The size of the labor force (twenty-five to sixty-four age group) is expected to increase by 18.9 percent in the United States, but the old-age dependency ratio will decrease to 94.4 percent in the United States. Richard Jackson, *The Global Retirement Crisis: The Threat to World Stability and What to Do about It* (Washington, D.C.: Center for Strategic & International Studies, April 2002).

33. Timothy Garton Ash, *The Uses of Adversity: Essays on the Fate of Central Europe* (New York: Vintage Books, 1989), p. 106.

34. President George W. Bush's comments at the NATO Summit in Istanbul are quoted in Anton La Guardia, *Daily Telegraph,* June 29, 2004, and Alec Russell, *Daily Telegraph,* June 30, 2004.

35. Richard Fletcher, *The Barbarian Conversion: From Paganism to Christianity,* op. cit., p. 304. Also, Tariq Ramadan, *To Be a European Muslim,* op. cit., p. 81.

36. S. George Ellsworth, "An Introduction," in *Utah's Road to Statehood,* edited by Bradford R. Cole and Kenneth R. Williams (Logan: Utah State University

Press, 1995). Kristen Moulton, "The Road to Utah's Statehood Wars Rocky," Associated Press, December 26, 1996.

37. Quoted in Rebecca Jones, "From the State of Flux to Statehood," in *Rocky Mountain News* (Denver, Colo.), July 27, 1999.

38. Gary Hufbauer and Frederic Neumann, "Conflict and Cooperation: The State of US-EU Trade and Investment Relations," SAIS Working Paper Series (WP/01/02), p. 4.

39. For a detailed and factual survey of the Euro-Atlantic economy, see Daniel S. Hamilton and Joseph P. Quinlan, *Partners in Prosperity: The Changing Geography of the Transatlantic Economy* (Washington, D.C.: Center for Transatlantic Relations, 2004).

40. This argument was first made in these words in the author's *Stay the Course: European Unity and Atlantic Solidarity* (Westport, Conn.: Praeger, 1997), p. 46.

41. Theodore H. White, *Fire in the Ashes*, op. cit., pp. 6–7.

42. Alain Minc, *Ce monde qui vient* (Paris: Grasset, 2004), pp. 1–43.

43. Andrew Moravcsik, ed., *Centralization or Fragmentation: Europe Facing the Challenges of Deepening, Diversity, and Democracy* (New York: Council on Foreign Relations, 1998), p. 6.

44. Marc F. Plattner, "Sovereignty and Democracy," *Policy Review* 122 (December 2003–January 2004), pp. 5–11.

45. Quoted in Myron P. Gilmore, *The World of Humanism, 1453–1517* (New York: Harper Colophon Books, 1952), p. 1.

46. Ludwig Dehio, *Germany and World Politics in the Twentieth Century* (New York: Alfred A. Knopf, 1959), p. 125.

47. Robert Legvold, "Russia," in *A Century's Journey*, edited by Robert A. Pastor (New York: Basic Books, 1999), p. 141.

48. Prime Minister Tony Blair's Speech to the Stock Exchange, Warsaw, Poland, October 6, 2000.

49. Henry A. Kissinger, *White House Years* (Boston: Little, Brown, 1979), p. 110.

50. Prime Minister Tony Blair's speech at the European Research Institute, Birmingham, November 23, 2001.

51. Samuel P. Huntington, quoted by Nicholas Lemann, "The Next World Order," *New Yorker*, April 1, 2002, p. 46.

52. Amitai Etzioni, *Political Unification Revisited: On Building Supranational Communities* (Lanham, Md.: Lexington Books, 2001), p. xxxi.

CHAPTER 5

1. Isaiah Berlin, *The Hedgehog and the Fox* (New York: Simon and Schuster, 1953), p. 19.

2. Raymond Aron, *Peace and War: A Theory of International Relations* (New York: Doubleday, 1966), p. 49.

3. Robert D. Kaplan, *Warrior Politics* (New York: Random House, 2002), p. 2.

4. Eliot A. Cohen, "History and the Hyperpower," *Foreign Affairs* 83, no. 4 (July/August 2004): 49–63.

5. Preface by Jean-Paul Sartre for Frantz Fanon, *The Wretched of the Earth*, translated by Constance Farrington (New York: Grove Press, 1963), pp. 7–34.

6. Bernard Lewis, "The Roots of Muslim Rage," in Fredrik Logevall, *Terrorism and 9/11: A Reader* (New York: Houghton Mifflin, 2002), pp. 5–20.

7. Paul Kennedy, *Preparing for the Twenty-First Century* (New York: Random House, 1993), pp. 14–15.

8. Quoted in Geir Kjetsaa, *Fyodor Dostoievsky: A Writer's Life* (New York: Viking, 1987), p. 252.

9. Samuel P. Huntington, *Political Order in Changing Societies* (New Haven, Conn.: Yale University Press, 1968), p. 196. Quoted in Jack Snyder, "Averting Anarchy in the New Europe," *International Security* 15, no. 3 (Winter 1990–1991).

10. John McCain, "There Is No Substitute for Victory," *Wall Street Journal*, October 26, 2001.

11. Paul Wolfowitz, "United on the Risks of a War with Iraq," *Washington Post*, December 23, 2002. Prepared statement, Hearings, Foreign Relations Committee, U.S. Senate, July 29, 2003. This echoes General MacArthur in September 1950, willing to accept unacceptable odds over the success of his landing at Inchon, a bold military move that changed the course of the Korean War, and, arguably, that of the Cold War—especially after a triumphant MacArthur next sought, with the same imprudent boldness to bring his army to the Yalu river, thereby starting a far more difficult war with the People's Republic of China.

12. As stated by President George W. Bush, in those words, on April 13, 2004.

13. See *The National Security Strategy of the United States of America* (Washington, D.C.: September 2002), including especially President Bush's opening letter, and his speeches at the National Cathedral (September 14, 2001), and West Point, New York (June 1, 2002).

14. Edward Luttwak, "Where Are the Great Powers?" *Foreign Affairs* 73 (July/August 1994): 23–28 and "Toward Post-Heroic Warfare," *Foreign Affairs* 74 (May/June 1995): 109–22.

15. Thomas Risse-Kappen, *Cooperation among Democracies*, op. cit., p. 16.

16. Christopher Layne, "The Unipolar Illusion: Why New Great Powers Will Rise," *International Security* 17, no. 4 (Spring 1993): 5–51.

17. Speech by Chris Patten, Cyril Foster Lecture, Balliot College, Oxford University, January 30, 2003.

18. A. J. P. Taylor, *Bismarck: The Man and the Statesman* (New York: Vintage Books, 1967), p. 13.

19. Robert W. Tucker and David C. Hendrickson, *The Imperial Temptation: The New World Order and America's Purpose* (New York: Council on Foreign Relations, 1992), p. 5.

20. Dulles's comments on brinksmanship are quoted in James Shepley, "How Dulles Averted War," *Life* (January 16, 1956).

21. Quoted in John Beale, *John Foster Dulles, 1989–1959* (New York: Harper & Row, 1959), p. 310.

22. For an early but still powerful presentation of this debate, see Robert W. Tucker, *Nation or Empire? The Debate over American Foreign Policy* (Baltimore: Johns Hopkins University Press, 1968).

23. From Secretary Acheson's remarks to the National Press Club, January 12, 1950, U.S. State Department *Bulletin*, vol. XXII, p. 114.

24. Condoleezza Rice, "Transforming the Middle East," *Washington Post*, August 7, 2003, and Address at the National Association of Black Journalists Convention, Dallas, Texas, August 7, 2003. See also, Ronald D. Asmus and Kenneth M. Pollack, "The New Transatlantic Project," *Policy Review* No. 115 (October–November 2002): 3–18.

25. Jeane Kirkpatrick, "Dictatorships and Double Standards," *Commentary*, vol. 68 (November 1979): 41.

26. The analogy built by the Bush administration between Iraq's condition in 2003 and Germany's reconstruction after 1945 is truly extraordinary. "The U.S. occupation [in Iraq] embraced that model [the 1945–1962 occupation of Germany] so completely that officials lifted whole passages from Marshall Plan—era documents in designing the future of Iraq." Michael Hirsh, "End Game," *Washington Post*, September 26, 2004.

27. Quoted in Gordon A. Craig, *The Germans*, op. cit., p. 45.

28. Paul Wolfowitz, quoted in James Mann, *Rise of the Vulcans*, op. cit., p. 136. See also Christopher Hitchens, "Aural History," *Atlantic Monthly* 291, no. 5 (June 2003): 100–101.

29. Goethe is quoted in Hans J. Morgenthau, *Scientific Man versus Power Politics* (Chicago: University of Chicago Press, 1948), p. 207.

30. Zbigniew Brzezinski, *Out of Control: Global Turmoil on the Eve of the 21st Century* (New York: Charles Scribner's Sons, 1993), pp. 100–101.

31. Carlo Levi, "Italy's Myth of America," *Life*, July 7, 1947, p. 84.

32. Quoted in Thomas Risse-Kappen, *Cooperation among Democracies*, op. cit., p. 157. See also Michael R. Beschloss, *The Crisis Years: Kennedy and Khrushchev, 1960–1963* (New York: HarperCollins, 1991), pp. 306–7.

33. Stefan Aust, Ralf Beste, and Gabor Steingart, Interview with Joschka Fischer, "America hatte kein Verdun," *Der Spiegel*, March 24, 2003.

34. Colin L. Powell, "A Strategy of Partnerships," *Foreign Affairs* 83, no. 1 (January 2004): 22–30.

35. Bernard Bailyn, *To Begin the World Anew* (New York: Alfred A. Knopf, 2003), p. ix.

36. See Philip H. Gordon and Jeremy Shapiro, *Allies at War: America, Europe, and the Crisis over Iraq* (Washington, D.C.: Brookings Institution, 2004), p. 199.

37. "They missed a good opportunity to be quiet," thundered Jacques Chirac of the ten countries that signed the Vilnius letter. Agence France-Presse, February 17, 2003.

38. Jean-François Revel, "Contradictions of the Anti-American Obsession," *New Perspectives Quarterly* 20, no. 2 (Spring 2003).

39. Ronald D. Asmus, Philip P. Everts, and Pierangelo Isernia, "Power, War, and Public Opinion," *Policy Review*, No. 123 (February 2004): 73–89.

40. Jeremy D. Rosner, "The Know-Nothings Know Something," *Foreign Policy*, no. 101 (Winter 1995/96): 116–30.

SELECTED
BIBLIOGRAPHY

Acheson, Dean. *Present at the Creation: My Years at the State Department* (New York: Norton, 1969).

Adler, Selig. *The Isolationist Impulse: Its Twentieth-Century Reaction* (New York: Free Press, 1957).

Albright, Madeleine. *Madam Secretary* (New York: Miramax Books, 2003).

Andréani, Jacques. *"Les Européens auront les Américains qu'ils méritent,"* *Commentaire* 94 (Summer 2001): 295–302.

Arendt, Hannah. *The Origins of Totalitarianism* (San Diego: Harcourt, Inc. 1995).

Armstrong, David. "Dick Cheney's Song of America," *Harper's Magazine* (October 2002): 76–83.

Aron, Raymond. *The Century of Total War* (Garden City, N.Y.: Doubleday, 1954).

——. *Peace and War: A Theory of International Relations* (New York: Doubleday, 1966).

——. *The Dawn of Universal History: Selected Essays from a Witness to the Twentieth Century*, translated by Barbara Bray (New York: Basic Books, 2002).

Ash, Timothy Garton. *The Uses of Adversity: Essays on the Fate of Central Europe* (New York: Vintage Books, 1989).

——. "The European Orchestra," *New York Review of Books*, May 17, 2001, pp. 60–66.

Asmus, Ronald D., and Kenneth M. Pollack. "The New Transatlantic Project," *Policy Review* 115 (October–November 2002): 3–18.

Asmus, Ronald D., Philip P. Everts, and Pierangelo Isernia. "Power, War, and Public Opinion," *Policy Review* 123 (February 2004): 73–89.

Asmus, Ronald D., James Dobbins, John Hulsman, et al. *One Year On: Lessons from Iraq*, Chaillot paper, no. 68 (Paris: Institute for Security Studies, March 2004).

Auriol, Vincent. *Mon Septennat, 1947–1954* (Paris: Gallimard, 1970).

Azéma, Jean Pierre. *1940, l'année terrible* (Paris: Editions du Seuil, 1990).

Bailyn, Bernard. *To Begin the World Anew: The Genius and Ambiguities of the American Founders* (New York: Alfred A. Knopf, 2003).

Balis, Christina, and Simon Serfaty, eds. *Visions of America and Europe: September 11, Iraq, and Transatlantic Relations*, (Washington, D.C.: CSIS Press, 2004).

Barraclough, Geoffrey. *An Introduction to Contemporary History* (Harmondsworth, U.K.: Penguin, 1967).

Barzini, Luigi. *The Europeans* (New York: Penguin Books, 1984).

Beale, John. *John Foster Dulles, 1989–1959* (New York: Harper & Row, 1959).

Berlin, Isaiah. *The Hedgehog and the Fox: An Essay on Tolstoy's View of History* (New York: Simon and Schuster, 1953).

———. *Four Essays on Liberty* (New York: Oxford University Press, 1969).

Beschloss, Michael R. *The Crisis Years: Kennedy and Khrushchev, 1960–1963* (New York: HarperCollins Publishers, 1991).

Brown, Seyom. *The Crises of Power: An Interpretation of United States Foreign Policy during the Kissinger Years* (New York: Columbia University Press, 1979).

Brzezinski, Zbigniew. *Out of Control: Global Turmoil on the Eve of the 21st Century* (New York: Charles Scribner's Sons, 1993).

———. *The Choice: Global Domination or Global Leadership* (New York: Basic Books, 2004).

Bullit, William C. *For the President, Personal and Secret: Correspondence between Franklin D. Roosevelt and William C. Bullit* (Boston: Houghton Mifflin, 1972).

Brogan, Denis W. *The American Character* (New York: Time Inc. Book Division, 1962).

Calleo, David P. *The Atlantic Fantasy: The U.S., NATO, and Europe* (Baltimore: Johns Hopkins University Press, 1970).

———. *Beyond American Hegemony: The Future of the Western Alliance* (New York: Basic Books, 1987).

Caraley, Demetrios James, ed. *The New American Interventionism: Lessons from Successes and Failures* (New York: Columbia University Press, 1999).

Carr, Edward H. *Nationalism and After* (London: Macmillan, 1968).

Carter, Jimmy. *Keeping Faith: Memoirs of a President* (New York: Bantam Books, 1982).

Chace, James. *Acheson* (New York: Simon & Schuster, 1998).

Clark, Wesley K. *Waging Modern War: Bosnia, Kosovo, and the Future of Combat* (New York: Public Affairs, 2001).

Cohen, Eliot A. "A Strange War," *National Interest*, no. 65 (Thanksgiving 2001): 11–23.

———. "History and the Hyperpower," *Foreign Affairs* 83, no. 4 (July/August 2004): 49–53.

Cole, Bradford R., and Kenneth R. Williams, eds. *Utah's Road to Statehood* (Logan: Utah State University Press, 1995).

Craig, Gordon A. *The Germans* (New York: Meridian Book, 1982).

Dehio, Ludwig. *Germany and World Politics in the Twentieth Century* (New York: Alfred A. Knopf, 1959).

Dinan, Desmond. *Europe Recast: A History of European Union* (Boulder, Colo.: Lynne Rienner Publishers, 2004).

Durant, Will and Ariel. *The Story of Civilization*, vol. VI, *The Reformation* (New York: Simon & Schuster, 1935).

Etzioni, Amitai. *The Monochrome Society* (Princeton, N.J.: Princeton University Press, 2001).

———. *Political Unification Revisited: On Building Supranational Communities* (Lanham, Md.: Lexington Books, 2001).

Fanon, Frantz. *The Wretched of the Earth*, translated by Constance Farrington (New York: Grove Press, 1963), Preface by Jean-Paul Sartre.

Ferguson, Niall. *Empire: The Rise and Demise of the British World Order and the Lessons for Global Power* (New York: Basic Books, 2003).

———. *Colossus: The Price of America's Empire* (New York: Penguin Press, 2004).

Fischer, Conan. *The Ruhr Crisis, 1923–1924* (Oxford: Oxford University Press, 2003).

Fletcher, Richard. *The Barbarian Conversion: From Paganism to Christianity* (New York: Henry Holt, 1997).

Gaddis, John Lewis. *We Now Know: Rethinking Cold War History* (Oxford, U.K.: Clarendon Press, 1997).

Garrison, Jim. *America as Empire: Global Leader or Rogue Power* (San Francisco: Berrett-Koehler Publishers, 2002).

Gelernter, David. "The Roots of European Appeasement," *Weekly Standard* 8, issue 2 (September 23, 2002).

Gilmore, Myron P. *The World of Humanism, 1453-1517* (New York: Harper Colophon Books, 1952).

Gordon, Philip H., and Jeremy Shapiro. *Allies at War: America, Europe, and the Crisis over Iraq* (Washington, D.C.: Brookings Institution, 2004).

Graebner, Norman A. *The New Isolationism: A Study in Politics and Foreign Policy since 1950* (New York: Ronald Press Co., 1956).

Greenfeld, Liah. *Nationalism: Five Roads to Modernity* (Cambridge, Mass.: Harvard University Press, 1992).

Grosser, Alfred. *Les Occidentaux* (Paris: Fayard, 1978).

Guérot, Ulrike. "The European Paradox: Widening and Deepening in the European Union," *U.S.-Europe Analysis Series*, Brookings Institution, June 2004.

Hamilton, Daniel S., and Joseph P. Quinlan. *Partners in Prosperity: The Changing Geography of the Transatlantic Economy* (Washington, D.C.: Center for Transatlantic Relations, 2004).

Habermas, Jurgen, and Jacques Derrida. "Europe: Plea for a Common Foreign Policy," translated by Douglas Gillison from its French version, *"Europe: plaidoyer pour une politique extérieure commune," Libération,* June 1, 2003.

Harrison, Michael M. *The Reluctant Ally: France and Atlantic Security* (Baltimore: Johns Hopkins University Press, 1981).

Harris, Lee. "The Intellectual Origins of America-Bashing," *Policy Review* 116 (December 2002/January 2003): 1-11.

Heisbourg, François. "How the West Could Be Won," *Survival* 44, no. 4 (Winter 2002-2003).

Heisbourg, François, vs. Charles Grant, "How Should Europe Respond to the New America," *Prospect Magazine* (April 2003): 16-20.

Hertsgaard, Mark. *The Eagle's Shadow: Why America Fascinates and Infuriates the World* (New York: Farrar, Straus and Giroux, 2002).

Hinsley, F. H. *Power and the Pursuit of Peace* (London: Cambridge University Press, 1963).

Hitchens, Christopher. "Aural History," *Atlantic Monthly* 291, no. 5 (June 2003): 100-101.

Hobsbawm, Eric, in conversation with Antonio Polito. *The New Century* (London: Little, Brown, 2000).

Hoffmann, Stanley, ed., *Conditions of World Order* (Boston: Houghton Mifflin Company, 1968).

Holcombe, Arthur N. "An American View of European Union," *American Political Science Review* 46 (1952).

Howard, Michael. "Mistake to Declare This a War?" *RUSI Journal* 146 (December 2001): 1–4.

Hufbauer, Gary, and Frederic Neumann, "Conflict and Cooperation: The State of US-EU Trade and Investment Relations," SAIS Working Paper Series (WP/01/02).

Hunter, Shireen, ed. *Islam: Europe's Second Religion* (Washington, D.C.: CSIS Press, 2002).

Huntington, Samuel P. *Political Order in Changing Societies* (New Haven, Conn.: Yale University Press, 1968).

——. "The U.S.—Decline or Renewal?" *Foreign Affairs* (Winter 1988–89): 76–97.

——. *The Clash of Civilizations and the Remaking of World Order* (New York: Simon & Schuster, 1996).

Hutton, Will. *The World We're In* (Boston: Little, Brown, 2002).

Ignatieff, Michael. *Empire Lite: Nation-Building in Bosnia, Kosovo, and Afghanistan* (New York: Penguin, 2003).

Ikenberry, G. John, ed. *American Foreign Policy: Theoretical Essays* (New York: Longman, 2005, 5th edition).

Isaac, Jeffrey C. *Arendt, Camus and Modern Rebellion* (New Haven, Conn.: Yale University Press, 1994).

Jackson, Richard. *The Global Retirement Crisis: The Threat to World Stability and What to Do about It* (Washington, D.C.: Center for Strategic & International Studies, April 2002).

Jervis, Robert. "The Compulsive Empire," *Foreign Policy* 137 (July/August 2003): 83–87.

Junker, Detlef. *The Manichean Trap: American Perceptions of the German Empire, 1871–1945*, German Historical Institute, Occasional Papers, no. 12 (1995).

Kagan, Robert. "The Benevolent Empire," *Foreign Policy* 112 (Summer 1998): 24–35.

——. *Of Paradise and Power: America and Europe in the New World Order* (New York: Vintage Books, 2004).

Kaplan, Robert D. *Balkan Ghosts: A Journey through History* (New York: Vintage Books, 1993).

——. *The Coming Anarchy: Shattering the Dreams of the Post Cold War* (New York: Random House, 2000).

——. *Warrior Politics: Why Leadership Demands a Pagan Ethos* (New York: Random House, 2002).

Keegan, John. *The First World War* (New York: Vintage Books, 1998).

Kennedy, Paul. *Preparing for the Twenty-First Century* (New York: Random House, 1993).

Kerry, Richard J. *The Star-Spangled Mirror: America's Image of Itself and the World* (Savage, Md: Rowman & Littlefield Publishers, 1990).

Kirkpatrick, Jeane. "Dictatorships and Double Standards," *Commentary* 68 (November 1979).

Kissinger, Henry A. *A World Restored* (Boston: Houghton Mifflin, 1973).

———. *White House Years* (Boston: Little, Brown and Company, 1979).

———. *Does America Need a Foreign Policy? Toward a Diplomacy for the 21st Century* (New York: Simon & Schuster, 2001).

Kjetsaa, Geir. *Fyodor Dostoievsky: A Writer's Life* (New York: Viking, 1987).

Kupchan, Charles. *The End of the American Era: U.S. Foreign Policy and the Geopolitics of the Twenty-First Century* (New York: Alfred A. Knopf, 2002).

———. "The End of the West," *Atlantic Monthly* 290, no. 4 (November 2002): 42–44.

Kurth, James. "The Adolescent Empire," *National Interest* 48 (Summer 1997): 3–15.

Laqueur, Walter. "America and the World: The Next Four Years," *Commentary* 63 (March 1977).

Layne, Christopher. "The Unipolar Illusion: Why New Great Powers Will Rise," *International Security* 17, no. 4 (Spring 1993): 5–51.

———. "America as European Hegemon," *National Interest* 72 (Summer 2003): 17–29.

Leites, Nathan. *The Rules of the Game in Paris* (Chicago: University of Chicago Press, 1969).

Lemann, Nicholas. "The Next World Order," *New Yorker* (April 1, 2002).

———. "Without a Doubt," *New Yorker* (October 14 and 21, 2002): 164–80.

Lévy, Bernard-Henry. "Anti-Americanism in the Old Europe," *NPQ* 20, no. 2 (Spring 2003): 5–10.

Lindbergh, Leon N., and Stuart A. Scheingold. *Europe's Would-Be Polity: Patterns of Change in the European Community* (Englewood Cliffs, N.J.: Prentice-Hall, 1970).

Lindley-French, Julian. *Terms of Engagement: The Paradox of American Power and the Transatlantic Dilemma, Post-11 September*, Chaillot Papers, no. 52, Institute for Security Studies (May 2002).

Lippmann, Walter. *The Cold War: A Study in U.S. Foreign Policy* (New York: Harper & Row, 1947).

Liska, George. *Imperial America* (Baltimore: Johns Hopkins University Press, 1967).

——. *War and Order: Reflections on Vietnam and History* (Baltimore: Johns Hopkins University Press, 1968).

——. *Beyond Kissinger: Way of Conservative Statecraft* (Baltimore: Johns Hopkins University Press, 1975).

Logevall, Fredrik, ed. *Terrorism and 9/11: A Reader* (New York: Houghton Mifflin, 2002).

Luttwak, Edward. "Where Are the Great Powers?" *Foreign Affairs* 73 (July/August 1994): 23–28.

——. "Toward Post-Heroic Warfare," *Foreign Affairs* 74 (May/June 1995): 109–22.

Macmillan, Harold. *At the End of the Day, 1961–1963* (New York: Harper & Row, 1973).

Macmillan, Margaret. *Paris 1919* (New York, Random House, 2003).

Mandelbaum, Michael. *The Dawn of Peace in Europe* (New York: Twentieth Century Fund, 1996).

Mann, James. *The Rise of the Vulcans: The History of Bush's War Cabinet* (New York: Viking Press, 2004).

May, Ernest R., and Philip D. Zelikow. *The Kennedy Tapes: Inside the White House During the Cuban Missile Crisis* (Cambridge, Mass.: Harvard University Press, 1997).

McCullough, David. *Truman* (New York: Simon & Schuster, 1992).

Mead, Walter Russell. *Special Providence: American Foreign Policy and How It Changed the World* (New York: Alfred A. Knopf, 2001).

Meunier, Sophie. "The French Exception," *Foreign Affairs* 79, no. 4 (July/August 2000): 104–16.

Miller, Linda B., and Michael J. Smith, eds. *Ideas and Ideals: Essays on Politics in Honor of Stanley Hoffmann* (Boulder, Colo.: Westview Press, 1993).

Milward, Alan. *The European Rescue of the Nation-State*, 2nd ed. (London: Routledge, 2000).

Minc, Alain. *Ce monde qui vient* (Paris: Grasset, 2004).

Miscamble, Wilson D. *George F. Kennan and the Making of American Foreign Policy, 1947–1950* (Princeton, N.J.: Princeton University Press, 1992).

Mitterrand, François. *Ici et maintenant* (Paris: Fayard, 1980).

Monnet, Jean. *Memoirs* (Garden City, N.Y.: Doubleday, 1978).

Moravcsik, Andrew, ed. *Centralization or Fragmentation: Europe Facing the Challenges of Deepening, Diversity, and Democracy* (New York: Council on Foreign Relations, 1998).

Morgenthau, Hans J. *Scientific Man versus Power Politics* (Chicago: University of Chicago Press, 1948).

Morris, Edmund. *Dutch: A Memoir of Ronald Reagan* (New York: Random House, 1999).

Niebuhr, Reinhold, ed. *Christian Realism and Political Problem* (New York: Scribner's, 1953).

Nye, Joseph S., Jr. *Bound to Lead: The Changing Nature of American Power* (New York: Basic Books, 1990).

——. *The Paradox of American Power: Why the World's Only Superpower Can't Go It Alone* (New York: Oxford University Press, 2002).

——. *Soft Power: The Means to Success in World Politics* (New York: Public Affairs, 2004).

Odom, William E., and Robert Dujarric. *America's Inadvertent Empire* (New Haven, Conn.: Yale University Press, 2004).

Packer, George. "War after the War," *New Yorker*, November 24, 2003.

Passeron, André. *De Gaulle Parle, 1962–1966* (Paris: Fayard, 1966).

Pastor, Robert A., ed. *A Century's Journey: How the Great Powers Shape the World* (New York: Basic Books, 1999).

Pauly, Robert J., Jr. *Islam in Europe: Integration or Marginalization* (Burlington, Vt.: Ashgate Publishing Company, 2003).

Peyrefitte, Alain. *C'était de Gaulle* (Paris: Fayard, 2000).

Pfeffer, Richard, ed. *No More Vietnams? The War and the Future of American Foreign Policy* (New York: Harper & Row, 1968).

Pipes, Richard. "Misinterpreting the Cold War: The Hardliners Had It Right," *Foreign Affairs* 73, no. 1 (January–February 1994).

Plattner, Marc F. "Sovereignty and Democracy," *Policy Review* 122 (December 2003–January 2004).

Podhoretz, Norman. *Making It* (New York: Random House, 1967).

——. *Present Danger* (New York: Simon and Schuster, 1980).

Powell, Colin L. "A Strategy of Partnerships," *Foreign Affairs* 83, no. 1 (January 2004): 22–30.

Quinlan, Joseph P. *Drifting Apart or Growing Together? The Primacy of the Transatlantic Economy* (Washington, D.C.: Center for Transatlantic Relations, 2003).

Ramadan, Tariq. *To Be a European Muslim* (London: Islamic Foundation, 1999).

Reid, Stuart. "The Anti-Europeans," *American Conservative*, January 27, 2003.

Revel, Jean-François. *L'obsession anti-américaine* (Paris: Plon, 2002).

——. "Contradictions of the Anti-American Obsession," *New Perspectives Quarterly* 20, no. 2 (Spring 2003).

Reynolds, David. "1940: Fulcrum of the Twentieth Century?" *International Affairs* 66, no. 2 (1990).

——, ed. *The Origins of the Cold War in Europe: International Perspectives*, (New Haven, Conn.: Yale University Press, 1994).

Rietbergen, Peter. *Europe: A Cultural History* (London: Routledge, 1998).

Rifkin, Jeremy. *The European Dream: How Europe's Vision of the Future Is Quietly Eclipsing the American Dream* (London: Penguin, 2004).

Risse-Kappen, Thomas. *Cooperation among Democracies: The European Influence on U.S. Foreign Policy* (Princeton, N.J.: Princeton University Press, 1995).

Rosecrance, Richard. "Croesus and Caesar: The Essential Transatlantic Symbiosis," *National Interest* 72 (Summer 2003): 31–34.

Rosner, Jeremy D. "The Know-Nothings Know Something," *Foreign Policy* 101 (Winter 1995/96).

Sbragia, Alberta M., ed. *Euro-Politics: Institutions and Policy-Making in the "New" European Community* (Washington, D.C.: Brookings Institution, 1992).

Schama, Simon. "The Unloved American," *New Yorker* 79, no. 3 (March 10, 2003): 54–60.

Schlossel, Lillian, ed. *The World of Randolph Bourne* (New York: E.P. Dutton & Co., 1965).

Schwartz, Benjamin, and Christopher Layne. "A New Grand Strategy," *Atlantic Monthly* 289, issue 1 (January 2002): 36–42.

Scott, George. *The Rise and Fall of the League of Nations* (New York: Macmillan Publishing Co., 1974).

Sebald, W. G. *On the Natural History of Destruction*, translated by Anthea Bell (New York: Modern Library, 1999).

Serfaty, Simon. "No More Dissent," *Foreign Policy* (Summer 1973): 144–58.

——. *Taking Europe Seriously* (New York: St. Martin's Press, 1992).

——. *Stay the Course: European Unity and Atlantic Solidarity* (Westport, Conn.: Praeger, 1997).

——. "Memories of Leadership," *Brown Journal of World Affairs* 5, no. 2 (Summer/Fall 1998): 3–16.

——. *La France vue d'Amérique: Réflexions sur la francophobie à Washington* (Paris: IFRI, 2002).

——, ed. *The European Finality Debate and Its National Dimensions* (Washington, D.C.: CSIS Press, 2003).

——. *La tentation impériale* (Paris: Odile Jacob, 2004).

Shennan, Andrew. *The Fall of France, 1940* (London: Pearson Education, 2000).

Sicherman, Harvey. "Where's the Rest of Me?" *Orbis* 44, no. 3 (Summer 2000).

Smith, Gaddis. *Morality, Reason and Power: American Diplomacy in the Carter Years* (New York: Hill and Wang, 1986)

Snyder, Jack. "Averting Anarchy in the New Europe," *International Security* 15, no. 3 (Winter 1990–1991).

Soros, George. *The Bubble of American Supremacy: The Costs of Bush's War in Iraq* (New York: Public Affairs, 2004).

Spaak, Paul-Henry. *The Continuing Battle: Memoirs of a European* (London: George Weidenfeld and Nicolson, 1971).

Steel, Ronald. *The End of Alliances: America and the Future of Europe* (New York: Viking Press, 1964).

——. *Pax Americana* (New York: Viking Press, 1967).

Tibi, Bassam. *The Challenge of Fundamentalism: Political Islam and the New World Disorder* (Berkeley: University of California Press, 1998).

Tucker, Robert W. *Nation or Empire? The Debate over American Foreign Policy* (Baltimore: Johns Hopkins University Press, 1968).

——. *The Inequality of Nations* (New York: Basic Books, 1977).

Tucker, Robert W., and David C. Hendrickson. *The Imperial Temptation: The New World Order and America's Purpose* (New York: Council on Foreign Relations, 1992).

Vagts, Alfred. "Battle and Other Combatant Casualties in the Second World War," *Journal of Politics* 7, no. 3 (1945).

Védrine, Hubert, with Dominique Moisi. *France in an Age of Globalization*, translated by Philip H. Gordon (Washington, DC: Brookings Institution, 2001).

Vertovec, Steven, and Cery Peach, eds. *Islam in Europe: The Politics of Religion and Community* (New York: St. Martin's Press, 1997).

Villepin, Dominique de. *Le requin et la mouette* (Paris: Plon, 2004).

Walker, Martin. "What Europeans Think of America," *World Policy Journal* 17, no. 2 (Summer 2000): 26–39.

Wallerstein, Immanuel. *Geopolitics and Culture: Essays on the Changing World-System* (Cambridge: Cambridge University Press, 1991).

Warner, Geoffrey. "Why the General Said No," *International Affairs* 78, no. 4 (2002): 869–83.

White, Theodore. *Fire in the Ashes: Europe in the Mid-Century* (New York: William Sloane Associates, 1953).

———. *In Search of History: A Personal Adventure* (New York: Warner Books, 1978).

Willetts, David, MP. *Old Europe? Demographic Change and Pension Reform* (London: Centre for European Reform, 2003).

Williams, William A. *The Tragedy of American History* (New York: Delta Books Publishing, 1962).

Woodward, Bob. *Bush at War* (New York: Simon & Schuster, 2002).

———. *Plan of Attack* (New York: Simon & Schuster, 2004).

Zelikow, Philip, and Condoleezza Rice. *Germany Unified and Europe Transformed: A Study in Statecraft* (Cambridge, Mass.: Harvard University Press, 1995).

Zweig, Stefan. *The World of Yesterday* (London: University of Nebraska Press, 1964).

INDEX

ABOUT THE AUTHOR

Simon Serfaty holds a senior professorship in international politics with the Graduate Programs in International Studies at Old Dominion University in Norfolk, Virginia, where he carries the university-wide title of Eminent Scholar. He also holds the Zbigniew Brzezinski Chair in Global Security and Geostrategy and serves as senior advisor to the Europe Program at the Center for Strategic and International Studies, a program he directed from 1994 to 2004. Previously, he taught at the University of California at Los Angeles and at the Paul H. Nitze School of Advanced International Studies of the Johns Hopkins University, where he held the positions of director of the Johns Hopkins Center of European Studies in Bologna, Italy, director of the Washington Center of Foreign Policy Research, and executive director of the Johns Hopkins Foreign Policy Institute.

Professor Serfaty's most recent book was written in French as *La tentation impériale* (Odile Jacob, 2004). His many books include *France, de Gaulle, and Europe* (1968), *The Elusive Enemy* (1972), *Fading Partnership* (1979), *American Foreign Policy in a Dangerous World* (1984), *Les années difficiles* (1986), *Taking Europe Seriously* (1992), *Stay the Course* (1997), and *Memories of Europe's Future: Farewell to Yesteryear* (2000). A naturalized citizen since 1965, he has also edited many other books including, most recently, *The European Finality Debate and its National Dimensions* (2003) and *Visions of America and Europe: September 11, Iraq, and Transatlantic Relations* (with Christina V. Balis, 2004).